THE SEA TROUT
AND THE FLY

THE SEA TROUT AND THE FLY

James Waltham

FOREWORD BY JOHN WILSHAW

THE CROWOOD PRESS

First published in 2006 by
The Crowood Press Ltd
Ramsbury, Marlborough
Wiltshire SN8 2HR

www.crowood.com

British Library Cataloguing-in-Publication Data
A catalogue record for this book is available from the British Library.

ISBN 1 86126 842 4
EAN 978 1 86126 842 6

The majority of the photographs in this book were taken by the author and John Wilshaw. Other photographic contributions were made by Paul Hopwood and Arthur Oglesby.

Frontispiece: The exception to the rule. This fine sea trout was taken on a Curry's Shrimp Fly while fishing for salmon. It is one of only a few sea trout that the author has caught using a shrimp pattern.

Typeset in Plantin by Bookcraft Ltd, Stroud, Gloucestershire

Printed and bound in Great Britain by The Cromwell Press, Trowbridge

Contents

For Jessica

Foreword

Sea trout, those enigmatic children of the tides, have long exercised the minds of our most innovative and enquiring anglers, and for good reason.

For the most part, sea trout fishing is practised during the hours of darkness, making it impossible to calculate how the quarry responds to our offerings. So how do we know, with any reasonable degree of certainty, if we are fishing the wrong fly at the wrong depth or speed? Worse still, how many of us have unwittingly snipped off the right fly at the wrong time!

Success, or lack of it, is also dependent on having an in-depth knowledge of a particular water. For instance, in Scotland and Ireland sea trout will often take freely in the daylight hours, especially if the water is carrying a tinge of colour. On the other hand, those in Wales who choose to fish for sea trout before day turns to night and the realm of bats and owls, are few.

On some rivers, a 1½–2in Black and Silver Waddington presented on a medium sinking line might be the first line of attack, while a floating line scratched across the surface of a dark pool on another river would be the preferred first choice. On other rivers, not that far distant, both methods might be regarded by local fishers as second-rate approaches. No doubt about it, each river has its own problems and peculiarities, its own flies and ways of fishing them.

Without the benefit of such vital local knowledge, the visiting angler will always be at a tremendous disadvantage. There will always be those nights when the sea trout refuse our best efforts no matter what we do. No sight is likely to frustrate yet at the same time spur the angler to try evcn harder, than the ranks of grey backs and swaying tails caught in the beam of a torch after many hours of fishing without the slightest of indications that the pool is home to even a single fish.

And so the addiction deepens its hold. James Waltham has suffered and succeeded and has caught a lot of sea trout in the process, often in conditions that would have defeated all but the most expert.

Happily, especially for those new to the pursuit of these mysterious princes of darkness, James has a knack of providing simple to understand solutions to what at first seem insurmountable problems. For many, this will be a bedtime story with the happiest of endings.

John Wilshaw

Acknowledgements

I am privileged to belong to this fly fishing fraternity – this bond of like-minded fanatics who, over many years, I have been fortunate enough to fish with and to learn from. Some are still going strong while others, alas, have gone to fish that great river in the sky.

I have heard it said that in the course of a lifetime a person's true friends can be counted on the fingers of one hand, and I don't doubt it. I must be one of the lucky ones for I am rich in true friends and, not surprisingly, most of them are anglers. I think of John Wilshaw of *Trout and Salmon*, who has been so encouraging and helpful to me while writing this book. Alf Gaskell, who now lives at Granton on Spey; we had some great fly-dressing times. Albert (get in the middle) Manfredi. Alistair (haddock man) Sinclair, Chairman of the Scottish Creelers and Divers Association (SCAD). Chris Slater, a very patient man and the world's best un-doer of knots. My son and best friend Chris, who can teach me a thing or two about sea fishing. Sid Knight, one of the greatest fly-dressers of all time and who I drove round the bend in the course of writing this book. Eddie Huyton, who can cast from the front at Southport and still land his bait in the sea. Michael Gilroy of Garrison, one of the great Irish fly fishermen and a believer in the 'little people'. Robert McHaffie, best known for his articles *Flies from Ireland*. Jim Helsby, my uncle, a great fisherman and mentor. Gavin Laidlaw, my dentist friend, who tries not to inflict too much pain. Dr Graham Smith, who it is always a pleasure to fish with. Getyhyn Thomas, a great fisherman and philosopher. Last, but by no means least, is my old and close friend Emelio Mutti, who is one of the most skillful and dedicated of sea trout anglers: what he doesn't know about sea trout fishing probably isn't worth knowing.

It is with much gratitude that I now mention Paul Hopwood and Karl Humphries, two dedicated sea trout fishermen and fly-dressers who have supplied me with many of the flies that are featured within these pages. Their unquestioned generosity and help has made the writing of this book all the more pleasurable.

Unfortunately, space prevents me from mentioning more, but those who I have not named will know who they are.

Preface

A good friend and keen sea trout fisherman once said to me that the only thing for certain about sea trout fishing is that nothing is for certain. There is an element of truth in this statement, for sea trout are arguably the most elusive and difficult of all game fish to catch. It is a fish that we still know relatively little about in scientific terms. There is no biological difference between a brown trout and a sea trout. Both are classified as *Salmo truffa*, which is often confusing as there is a vast difference in the behaviour of the two species. The sea trout migrates to sea where, like its close relative the salmon, it takes on a silver appearance and, again like the salmon, returns to its native river to spawn. The brown trout, on the other hand, remains as a permanent resident. Why some migrate to sea and others do not remains a mystery. Sea trout are arguably the most powerful and hard fighting of all game fish, which is why catching them is all that more rewarding, especially on a fly: the ultimate goal. While it may be true that nothing is for certain in this fascinating branch of the sport, to be armed with as much knowledge as possible will only serve to increase your chances of pleasure and success.

Fly fishing is so often a sport of lost opportunities and 'what ifs'. How often have you returned from an unsuccessful fishing session, sat down in the armchair, or perhaps lost sleep, tossing over in your mind what might have been? What if I had tried the fly that so-and-so gave me? What if I had used a sinking line instead of a floater – the fish were probably deep down. If only. What if I…? And occasionally the penny seems to drop and you think you know where you went wrong. I'll try that fly of Bill's next time – bound to work. And when it does you have the satisfaction of having solved yet another problem, in reaching the next rung on the ladder of learning. To be able to catch sea trout with consistency can often take years of experimenting and searching for knowledge. It is much like learning music. The beginner starts by learning his or her basic keys, the bars and shapes of notes, the correct tempo and so on, until at last the music can be read without too much effort and a good tune is played. The same could be said for most forms of fishing; the angler learns his skill to a point when he catches his quarry with regularity, like learning to ride a bike. But when it comes to sea trout fishing, the angler, in comparison, must be capable of conducting an orchestra. Such is the requirement to become proficient, for sea trout seldom conform in the way we would wish. They can often prove unpredictable and frustrating to catch. After years of experience a good conductor will have a feeling for the mood, the passion and the intention of the composer. He has rehearsed with the orchestra until he is fully aware of the capabilities of each musician and has brought out the best in them. And then, when the hall is still and he raises his baton to begin he is confident that great music will ensue.

And so, as I sit down to write this book, I ask myself why I have set out on this mission. Is it for money? I doubt it – it isn't like writing a best-selling novel. I write this book because I wish to share my experiences with you and hope that by doing so I will help you to shorten the journey, gain more knowledge and consequently catch more sea trout. I will try, at least, to teach you some of the music, but as with any skill, proficiency will only come with practice. If you are a novice, or have never fished for sea trout before, then I hope that this book will give you encouragement. But equally as important, I hope to give you confidence, which is a key element to successful fishing.

If you are already an experienced sea trout angler, you may find something of interest, in as much as I am always learning something new myself. If you are not an angler, yet find this book interesting, I will have achieved more than I dared to hope.

James Waltham
January 2005

The author choosing the right fly, with a little help from a friend.

Introduction

It seems that I have always been crazy about fishing in one form or another. Just like the rest of the men in my family before me who were all fanatical anglers, I was no exception. It could, and has, been said that I was born with the 'bug'. When I was only a toddler my grandad fixed a little wooden seat to the crossbar of his bike so that he could take me fishing with him. On the local reservoir he taught me all the basic skills of course fishing: how to balance the float with lead shot, how to ledger and what baits to use for each particular kind of fish and much more. Through his teaching I became fascinated by the countryside, the ever-changing landscape, the birds and animals, but most of all the fish. Pike and perch, roach and bream, gudgeon and eels all became sources of wonderment and the origin of a hobby that would last for the rest of my life.

By the time I was twelve, my Uncle Jim had acquired a motorbike and side-car. Few people had cars then and even a motorbike with a side-car was something of a status symbol. Each Sunday morning he would call round to take me fishing. I was so keen to get going that I used to stand and stare through the window for a good hour or more before he arrived. I must have been the envy of all the other kids on our estate, who would always gather round to admire the gleaming 500 Norton and watch me squeeze into the side-car amongst all the tackle. Then we were off, usually to some remote and exciting part of the Scottish Lowlands in search of big pike.

My life as a fly fisherman, however, began when I was a teenager in those far-off days of long balmy summers and even longer freezing winters. But as long as the summers may have been, they always ended far too quickly, bringing an end to the fishing until the following spring. As a boy there was never much to do through the long, cold, winter months. Loitering outside the local chip shop with the lads was the usual thing. It seemed warmer here on those cold evenings and the smell was good too. And if you had a tanner (six pence, old money) to spend you could buy a big poke of chips and a scallop soaked in vinegar, but more often than not we were moved on by the short-tempered proprietor. Little seems to have changed to this day. There was always football of course, except we rarely had a ball to kick, it was usually a tin can. The game was kick-can lurkey, played up the dark alleyways. Strange, now I think about it, I can still hear the clatter of the can being kicked the length of McGinty's cobbled alley by the two opposing teams of rough and noisy kids, and the gruff tone of big Mrs Cameron (the dragon) bawling what she was going to do if she caught us playing football up her back passage again. She never could understand why we would all run off in fits of laughter as she stood shaking her fist after us. 'Go on, bugger off or I'll get the police.' On rainy nights we would wander into the musty, church hall youth club with its torn snooker table with half the balls missing. Or there was table tennis, except the table had no net. As if that wasn't enough, there was the attendant inebriate minister to put up with. He went on and on about why we should attend church on Sundays and threatened hell and damnation if we didn't.

Saturday, however, was a day to look forward to. I would take a bus ride into the big town, where I would spend the best part of my pocket money in the record shop on the latest Number One. If there was any change I would buy a copy of the *Angling Times*. It was all Elvis, Chuck Berry and Buddy Holly in those days, which tells you how long ago it was.

Spring, and time to go fishing again, could never arrive quickly enough. It was a time when the whole world seemed to come alive. I always looked forward to Grand National Day – that was when I knew that spring had finally arrived. The Oxford and Cambridge Boat Race the following week confirmed it. Time again to take another look at my fishing tackle, for what it was worth, and to plan how I was going to catch Moby Dick, the legendary giant pike that lived in Percy's Dub. They said it was a world record size and that plenty had hooked it but none had ever landed it. Maybe this year that honour would go to me – after all, I had been taught a thing or two about pike fishing. Not only that, Farmer Percy had offered a big reward to anyone who caught it.

I have fond memories of the spring days when our gang of scruffs would cycle up to the dub to catch perch, using worms dug from the park compost heap. Those who were lucky enough to have more than one rod would fish the second rod with a dead bait and a big cork bung to tempt Old Moby, but he never obliged. I found out some years later that Moby Dick had never even existed, it was all a big lie invented by that sly old farmer to attract a lot of gullible kids. This way it was easier for him to find recruits to help with the potato picking.

No Hardy rods for us. Ours were hand-me-downs of bamboo or greenheart with half the rings missing. Floats were made from ostrich quills and rubber bands, and to sustain us

through the day we usually had a bottle of flat warm pop and two rounds of spam butties. Rain or shine, we would fish all day until we were ravenous, then it was home to Mum's homemade tripe and onions, or meat and potato pie and chips on a good day.

As spring turned to summer, and I turned fourteen, I was looking forward to the summer holiday. Seven whole weeks off school. This, however, would be a special summer. My Uncle Wullie, who netted salmon for a living on the estuary of the River Forth, had said that I could spend the holidays with him and help with the netting as Archie, his assistant, had broken his leg. This, I found out later, was not quite true. Archie, being a hard drinker and part-time poacher, had, while under the influence, gaffed himself in the leg while attempting to snatch a salmon from the River Teith.

It seemed that summers really were long and warm then, for we would work all through the night wearing nothing more than a pair of shorts. I soon got the hang of operating the nets. Starting at dusk, when the salmon would swim in closer to the shore, we would row out, paying the long net behind us. A circle was formed to surround the fish before returning to shore. Here we would climb out into the mud and weed, where we would slip and slide like a pair of mudlarks, laughing at each other as we hauled in the net. It was extremely hard work but I loved every moment of it. I can remember the excitement of seeing those bars of silver as the net came closer in. One night we caught fourteen salmon and six sea trout in one haul, which put a broad smile on Uncle Wullie's face and, for my efforts, I received an extra four pounds for that night's work, which to me was a fortune in those days. I was suddenly rich.

When Friday arrived, I was told that we wouldn't be netting that night. Instead, we were going to do some real fishing. I wasn't sure what he meant by that, but I looked forward with curiosity to whatever was in store. After a late dinner, which Uncle Wullie seemed to take forever to eat, we set off in his battered Land Rover. He told me that there had been rain on the hills and the prospects were good to fish the River Allan for sea trout. But it was too early just yet to fish for sea trout, he explained, that was best after dark. He would first show me something interesting to kill the time.

He pulled in by the edge of a boulder-strewn bog, where he tackled up two fly rods – one for him, one for me – each with a small dry fly on the point. Ignoring the DANGER KEEP OUT signs, we set off over the moor until at length we arrived at what had once, in another age, been a quarry. Following his lead, I quietly crept to the edge and peered over the sheer rock face. Far below us, some fifty feet or more, was a dark deep lagoon.

'See them rising?'
Yes, I could see the rings all over the black surface.

'Have ye ever caught a troot on a flea?' he asked.
I told him I hadn't. I had never even held a fly rod before.

'Ye will now. Lower yer line doon.'

We held our rods out over the edge and began to pull line off the reel. The flies slowly descended until they touched the surface, and immediately both flies were siezed by greedy brown trout. Following a short tussle, our prizes were reeled the long assent up the quarry face. They were not big fish by any imagination, perhaps a half pound apiece, but they were beautiful objects of precious gold with big red spots. And I had caught my first fish on a fly.

As the day faded into dusk we were on the river. I was told that it was in perfect condition and full of fish. I was handed a small fly box, which on opening I discovered contained about fifty flies, all the same pattern but in various sizes. They were all Alexanders, but Uncle Wullie's own variation, and apparently

the only sea trout fly he ever used. He told me where to stand on the edge of the shingle and instructed me to keep on casting towards the opposite bank, which I could now barely see. I began to thrash away at the river, not really knowing what I was doing, while my good uncle, who was now intent on some serious fishing, and no doubt didn't wish to waste too much time on this little squirt, made his way a short distance upstream leaving me to my own devices.

Before long there was a commotion on the surface. 'Jim' he called. 'Come and net this.'

I did. It was a beauty of about 4lb. I had mixed feelings of awe and envy. I imagined he must be the greatest angler in the world. Oh how I wanted to catch one myself.

I wandered back down the river to try again. Eventually, I somehow managed to cast the line across the pool. I was beginning to get the hang of it – sort of. Suddenly it was as if I had received an electric shock. The whack as a big sea trout grabbed the fly. And then, in the blinking of an eye, the fish was gone and I stood there, nerves tingling, wondering if I had imagined it. I never connected with another fish that night, although Uncle Wullie caught six more, which I netted for him. I was left with a great desire, a passion even, to catch a sea trout. Anyone could net them. I wanted to catch one on a fly.

He promised to take me again the following Friday. So for the next six days I spent as much time as I could on the local football field, practising to cast. I couldn't wait to try again. The week passed painfully slow. But at last Friday evening arrived and as we set off for the river I was filled with excitement and anticipation. I was determined that this would be the night.

As the sun began to fall away behind the hills, fish began to show in the pools and I anxiously tied on one of Uncle Wullie's Alexanders. I was feeling confident now that I had learned to cast, albeit in an amateurish fashion, and was itching to get started.

INTRODUCTION

'Wait a wee while,' came the advice. 'It's no dark enough yet.' My uncle sat down and lit a pipe while I sat twiddling with the rod. It seemed that it would never get dark enough, but eventually he knocked his pipe out on a rock and got up. 'Ye can start now,' he said, as he made his way upstream. I stayed where I was: this was the spot where I had lost the fish the previous Friday. I was sure to catch one here.

I persevered for about two hours without any luck, but at least I didn't have to keep stopping to net Uncle Wullie's fish. He had wandered too far upstream, but I was sure he had caught one or two by now – lucky thing. But, no, he wasn't lucky, he was just good at it. I'd be as good as him one day. I'd show him. Little did I realise just how many years that was going to take me.

I didn't quite care for being left alone in the middle of the night and by now I was feeling a little uneasy about it. Each rustle in the grass was beginning to send shivers down my spine. What if it was a giant rat, or a snake even? I didn't care much for those bats that were flitting about either. What if they were vampires? The hair on the back of my neck was beginning to stand on end. Spooky. I should never have listened to those stories about Count Dracula.

Just as I was wishing I was somewhere else, a sea trout splashed a little further down the pool. Thoughts of giant rats and snakes were forgotten. I walked down a little and cast towards where I thought I had seen the fish move. The fly was immediately taken. It was on and tearing fine off the reel as it rushed upstream. Please don't let me lose it. It was fighting like mad. It must be a monster. Wow! It ran all over the place before it started to weaken and I gingerly brought it closer and closer towards me. Oh no. I hadn't been provided with a landing net. No doubt my Uncle didn't give much for my chances of catching anything and had wandered off with the only net. The fish was now thrashing away by my feet and I was sure it would escape. Desperation. And then some ghostly dark object seemed to pass beneath my fish and suddenly it was in the air. My Uncle had arrived in the nick of time and netted it.

It wasn't the monster I had imagined; it weighed 2lb, but it was mine. I will always remember that feeling of elation and pride when he slapped me on the back. 'Well done laddie. Well done.'

I was now a sea trout fisherman – or so I imagined. The journey had only just begun.

Time to get ready. Perfect conditions on a low and clear pool at dusk.

1 Preparing for the Night

Most sea trout fishing is done on rivers under the cover of darkness. This is not because sea trout anglers are secretive people, but because this is usually the time when fish are most active and therefore easier to catch. Fly fishing is usually most productive when the river is low and clear or, at least, falling towards its normal summer level after a good downpour, which has encouraged fish to run upstream. These are the fish that will oblige in the dark. Unless the river is running high and coloured they will be much more difficult, but not impossible, to catch by day. They will be well hidden under overhanging trees or under larger stones. When no such cover is available they will take advantage of their amazing camouflage against the river bed where they lie motionless, often in large shoals. The only tell-tale sign of their presence is when one occasionally flips to reveal its silver flank. So, if you intend to fish through the night, it makes good sense to know exactly where the fish are lying. Consequently, some daylight reconnaissance will be essential before you begin.

You should arrive early when there is plenty of light left in the day. Wear clothes that will blend in with the background and be equipped with a good pair of polarised glasses. Move slowly as you go along the bank. Your movements should be in slow motion even. Sudden movement will cause such easily spooked fish to scatter. Stop at each likely fish-holding place and wait a while. Try not to stand in the open or too close to the edge and take advantage of any cover offered by the riverside vegetation. Quite often, especially in those deeper pools, sea trout are not instantly visible. Allow your eyes time to adjust to the light and shade. What at first you might think are stones or patches of weed will often be fish lying close to the bottom. The best and easiest places to fish are where you are less likely to get snagged in overhanging branches, and if you must wade, get a good idea what the bed of the river is like. All of this might seem like stating the obvious, but I have often seen anglers who thought that such a softly softly approach was not important.

I recall arriving on the bank of the River Irt in Cumbria late one August afternoon, with the intention of fishing through the night. As I parked up in the lay-by by the bridge, another angler, who was dressed in a bright yellow anorak, was in the process of tackling up. We exchanged a few brief words about the weather and the price of petrol. Then, after a while, and after having assessed that I was a trustworthy sort of bloke, he asked me if I would mind looking after his tackle while he went on a quick recce. By this, he meant fish spotting. 'No problem' I told him. 'Take your time.' It was far too early to start fishing yet anyhow. I watched him go upstream like a bull in a china shop, standing close to the edge of each pool as he gawked at the water. At the third pool he actually picked up a stick and began thrashing away at the reeds to get a better look. Perhaps he was expecting the fish to shout 'We're

15

here mate.' I was determined I would fish downstream.

He returned within fifteen minutes wearing a glum expression and I wasn't surprised when he told me that fishing would be a waste of time.

'How's that?' I asked, knowing what the answer would be.

'No fish. Nothing. And I've come all the way from Burnley.'

'It's full of fish,' I told him, 'Look.' I pointed to the large pool by the edge of the road, a pool which, thankfully, he had not bothered to ruin. He gave me a look that suggested I was a bit simple in the head. 'Try these.' I handed him my Polaroids, which he put on.

'Bloody hell. You're right.' The pool was full of fish.

'Have you ever watched that TV programme, Kung Fu?' I asked him. 'You know, the one where the guy walks on rice paper.' He didn't get it. He gave me another curious look, gathered up his tackle and, thankfully, headed off up the river. But I wouldn't mind betting that it wasn't long before he bought himself a pair of Polaroids. I wonder if he caught anything?

So good reconnaissance is, of course, vital to the sea trout angler. There is more to this, however, than having a nice stroll along the river before it goes dark, and although it is important to know exactly where the fish are, it is just as important to know exactly where you are. You have walked your chosen beat and made mental notes of how the current flows, or where those overhanging bushes are, or where the path meanders, or where the best place is to cross that barbed wire fence without ripping your waders. A lot to take in, but beware. The scene which you have tried to memorise by day can appear totally different in the dark.

I once went to fish on the Cumbrian Esk as the guest of a well-known TV presenter and writer. It was a stretch of river that I had often fished and thought I knew well. But on this occasion I was to find out just how important it is to arrive early and to familiarise yourself with the scene. I had arrived late, just as darkness was falling. I said a quick hello and tried to make a fast exit without appearing rude. I just wanted to get on the river bank, but my host insisted I first shared a glass (or two) of whisky with him. How could I refuse? By the time I got away it was pitch dark, one of the darkest nights I can remember.

Even in daylight it can sometimes be difficult to find your way down to the river through the sloes and shrub-covered mounds, but I remembered the way without too much effort and was soon fishing on the bottom pool, where I took three nice sea trout in no time at all.

Later into the night I decided to try my luck in a higher pool, but to get there I had to go round a thicket surrounding a bog, which had now become overgrown. I had often followed this track and knew it well; or so I thought. I wandered up the river through the tall reeds, then cut through the dense sloes to pick up the track, except there was no track to find. I ventured a little further into some hostile undergrowth, which was now getting thicker. Surely the track was here somewhere. It wasn't. I was soon entangled in brush and brambles so dense that I was literally having to fight my way through while receiving a thousand scratches and countless nettle stings. That's when my foot suddenly sank into a deep trench. I lost my balance and fell headlong into the brambles, and disaster. I heard that sickening crack as I landed on my rod. The night's fishing was over. I wonder if the whisky played any part in my misadventure?

I had a similar experience on the River Ribble one dark August night. I had walked downstream from the bridge to fish a likely

Imagine fishing here at night. Good daytime reconnaissance would be essential.

at the water's edge in a dishevelled state. I fished until about 3am, when it was time to go. I had important matters to see to later in the day and thought it wise to get at least a few hours sleep. Even with the help of a torch I was unable to find the path that I had forced through that dreadful jungle. The darkness plays strange tricks. If only I had marked my exit somehow. To escape I had two options. I could wade downstream through the long rapids or wade upstream through some deep and potentially dangerous water. I chose the former but it still took a good hour or more before I eventually arrived at my car. I might just as well have fished on until first light.

An idea later occurred to me, an idea which I now use frequently to prevent such things happening again. I now carry a small aerosol of white florist's paint.

The following week I returned to the pool on the Ribble and again hacked my

pool that sits above a long series of rapids. These run for the best part of a quarter of a mile. Having pushed up through this long stretch of fast water, sea trout and salmon will almost certainly stop to rest here for a while. As I approached the pool I was troubled to find that the bank had become so overgrown with knot weed, hog weed and all kinds of other vegetation that it was impossible to see the pool, which I guessed was some seventy-five yards away on the other side. I searched for some time to find a way through, but found none. I would have to create my own path. After about fifteen minutes of hacking and applied brute force I eventually emerged

A productive stretch of the River Ribble near Waddington.

way through the vegetation. But this time I marked the exit and found my way back without too much effort. In addition, a dead tree stump by that unforgettable swamp in Eskdale soon had three white stripes sprayed on it to remind me to keep to the right of it when next making my way upstream on a black night.

One early September evening I went to fish a stretch on the River Lune near Kirkby Lonsdale with my good friend and expert sea trout angler, Emelio Mutti. Neither of us had fished that particular stretch before and we were keen to give it a try. But it had been a scorching day and as we turned off the M6 and neared Caton we both decided that our thirsts had to be tamed. We stopped at the Station Hotel and enjoyed a nice cool pint of shandy before continuing on our way. This, however, meant that we arrived later in the evening than we had planned, but there was still enough light to go on an explorative walk.

We made our way down from the old bridge, passing some likely looking runs while noting that some good sea trout were already beginning to make themselves known. As this was a new water to us we wanted to take in as much of the stretch as we could and continued walking towards where a pipe-track crosses the river. Just above this pipe-track was a cracking looking streamy run that was impossible to fish due to the steep rocky bank and the overhanging trees. But it did look fishable from the opposite bank.

Emelio decided to fish the long shallow run just below the pipe-track, but I was determined to fish the run above it and, although the river is wide here, I waded across and made my way back upstream.

From this side the run looked even better, with an easily fishable shingle shore. But getting down to it was another matter. The clay bank was some ten feet above the water's edge, crumbling away in parts,

and had a very steep drop. It hadn't looked this difficult from the other side, but here I was and nothing was going to stop me now. Yes, the grass is always greener and will probably remain so. This was going to prove a challenge as I could see only one precarious route down. I slid, rather than climbed, down until I crunched the shingle. This would have been a daft thing to do on any occasion, but with a bag, a rod and a landing net to contend with it was an act of madness. However, I was down and ready to fish, but being aware that I would later have to get back up in the dark, I took out the aerosol, and the appropriate places that offered a grip and a toe hold were duly

The author fishing one of his favourite Lakeland streams where double-figure sea trout can be expected.

anointed. I was thankful I had because the night turned as black as ink. I did get back up but I have to admit it took a great deal more effort than it did getting down, especially with the extra weight of three fat sea trout in the bag.

Another occasion when the aerosol spray came in useful was when fishing on the River Annan. One of my favourite pools follows a gentle curve, with fine gravel to walk on. It slopes gradually away into deeper water under the far bank, which is shaded by a steep tree-covered hill; a perfect lie for sea trout. Part way down the pool, however, a dead tree stuck out into the water from the

The famous Wheel Hole Pool on the Cumbrian Leven. The faster water running through the middle of the pool will hold salmon, while sea trout prefer to lie under the trees close to the bank.

opposite bank. It had been there for years and I should have been well aware of it. I had been caught up on it on a couple of previous occasions and this particular night was no exception. Another good fly was lost and again that obstacle was cursed. But this time I had the aerosol can with me. No, I didn't swim across and spray the dead tree; I found three larger stones, which I sprayed and set down on the gravel opposite the dead tree. Now each time I fished in the pool I was reminded to stand a couple of yards further back before casting. It worked a treat and no further flies were lost, at least not on that tree.

One last and important tip for use of the aerosol is to make a mark close to the river level you are fishing at; a horizontal line on a rock is ideal for telling you if the river is rising or falling. This could even save your life.

I remember fishing on the River Ribble one August night in 2002. The river was in perfect condition for fly fishing and I took a nice fish almost as soon as it was dark. Shortly after, Emelio, who had waded a good way out – the river is wide here – and was stood up to his waist in a good glide some two hundred yards below me, hooked and lost a rather big fish, which he thought might have been a salmon rather than a sea trout. Emelio is something of an expert at catching salmon in the dark.

By midnight I was starting to feel the drop in temperature so decided it was time for a cuppa. I sat on a big rock, took out my flask and poured a hot and welcome coffee. Lovely. I was feeling warmer already; what could be nicer, another fish perhaps? Maybe even a record sea trout, or perhaps Emelio's lost salmon might come back for another go and take my fly. Dream on. I finished the coffee and thought how nice another one would be so I reached for the flask once more and was surprised when my hand touched water. I looked for the

PREPARING FOR THE NIGHT

(Left) The author fishing the Golden Grove beat on the River Towy. Here the river is subject to frequent change after winter flooding. (Right) A crumbling bank on the River Clwyd. Soil banks such as this one are continuously eroded by flooding, and the character of the river and its pools are subject to change from season to season. Shortly after this picture was taken the bank collapsed under the weight of a cow, which fortunately managed to scramble out unhurt.

white line, it had vanished. Rivulets of water were now running like quicksilver between the rocks: a flash flood! I jumped up and yelled to Emelio, who seemed oblivious to what was going on, to get out of the water quick. We both made it to the high bank before a deluge of water swept on past us. Although the sky was overcast, the weather had seemed settled, with no hint of any rain – not here at least. But higher up the valley, around Settle, there had been a very heavy cloudburst. I think we may have been lucky on that occasion for within the next hour we watched the river rise by at least four feet before we made tracks.

Although the aerosol can be a useful tool, please don't go mad with it. There are enough stupid graffiti artists in the towns. Use it sparingly so that you do not annoy a farmer or your fellow anglers.

You never step into the same river twice; the only thing that is constant along the river is change.
Kenny Salwey (*Mississippi River Rat*)

If you are making your first trip of the season to the river then beware. Although you think you might have a good mem-ory of the banks and water course from the previous season, you might be in for a surprise. Floods, particularly over the winter and spring, will often erode banks and change pools and runs beyond recognition. I remember once going up to the border to fish the River Esk (not to be confused with the Cumbrian Esk). I had arrived too late to survey the beat – it was almost dark. But no problem, I had fished here quite a number of times over the previous season. I knew my way along this stretch well enough, but as I approached what had been one of my favourite pools, I was wondering if I had come to the right place. Perhaps I was loosing my marbles. The main current, which had once ran on the opposite side, now ran under my feet and that shingle, which had sloped gradually away making casting very easy indeed, was now piled high against the opposite bank. Had I crossed the wrong field perhaps? Surely not. I remembered that white gate. It had to be the right place. I made my way downstream to discover that the character of the whole beat had altered. This may be an exceptional example but, nevertheless, river banks and current flows frequently change.

To emphasise the point, a friend went up to fish the River Whitadder above Duns. Thinking he knew that particular bit of river well, he spent the earlier part of the evening in the pub enjoying a good meal, and who could blame him. The landlord, Nigel, who, with regret, no longer keeps that pub, is a chieftain amongst chefs. His Aberdeen Angus steaks were something to die for – and my friend almost did.

It was dark when he finally arrived at his favourite pool. As usual, he started by fishing his way down the fast run at the top of the pool but, unknown to him, winter and spring floods had gouged a deep rut at the bottom end of the run and before he knew it he was up to his chin in the fast-flowing river. Had it not been for an overhanging branch, which he was able to grab on to, who knows what might have become of him. So get there early.

Low and clear summer conditions on the River Dulus near Machynlleth in mid-Wales. To the untrained eye, pools like this one can appear empty of fish by day but will boil with sea trout once the sun has gone down.

2   Things of the Night

This is a subject seldom touched on by writers on sea trout fishing, but one that I thought would do no harm in raising here. Human beings are by nature a superstitious breed. We have an ingrained fear of the unknown based on a number of factors, such as religious beliefs or childhood stories of the bogie man, which, although most would be reluctant to admit, is carried in our subconscious minds for our entire lives. So it may not be surprising to learn that a good many anglers are not too keen on the idea of fishing alone in the middle of nowhere at night. I once knew a tough rugby player who was well known for his aggression on the field but who, although he enjoyed his sea trout fishing, would never venture far from the roadside, preferring to fish only under the lights on the bridge. I also knew another angler who wore a large crucifix dangling about his neck. The reason was obvious as he never wore it during the day. Another angler would only fish at night in the close company of a friend. Some anglers are more honest and will readily admit that they would never consider the thought of fishing alone in the dark.

After reading one of my articles in a certain fly fishing magazine, a reader wrote to me about his own frightening, and indeed disturbing, experience.

The man (let's call him Tom) had arranged to meet up with a friend on the bank of the river for a spot of sea trouting. It was almost dark when the meeting took place but, after the usual pleasantries, it was agreed that Tom would fish the beat downstream while his friend fished upstream.

As the hours passed, Tom, who was stood up to his waist in the middle of the river, felt a gentle bump against the back of his leg. Nothing surprising about that. Branches, logs and other debris being carried downstream are often the cause of the bump in the night. But on this occasion it had been no log that had bumped poor Tom; it had

A 'haunted' pool on the Lanhydrock Estate water on the River Fowey in Cornwall. This is the very pool where I went for a dip (see 'Goggle Eyed Demon').

been the body of his friend who had suffered a fatal heart attack and had drifted down the river. Tom has not fished alone at night since.

I heard from a friend about his own dreadful experience when fishing alone one night on the River Conwy below Betws-y-coed. It had been a dark September night, with on and off drizzle to add to the misery of a fishless session. By about 2am, when Tony was feeling tired and fed up and was thinking about a warm bed, something brushed against his leg. Not a log, or a fertiliser bag, or even a fish, but something frighteningly cold and macabre. What was it? A sense of foreboding swept over him. As he stared into the water the large hump of some strange creature broke the surface, swirled in the current, then plunged to the bottom. Tony was concerned to say the least. Was it just his imagination? Of course it was. The night was teasing him; it must have been a branch or something like that. He tried to pull himself together and dispel such silly notions. But then, as he continued to search the surface, an evil, disgusting, slime-covered face floated up. He stared into the eyes of something so hideous that it had to be a creature from the very depths of hell. Then the smell caught his nostrils. The sickly putrid smell of death cut through the air like a knife.

He ran. He ran like his life depended on it and, as far as Tony was concerned, it did. He threw his tackle in the car and prayed that the engine of his old banger would start. It did. Thank God. He put his foot to the floor and didn't stop until he arrived an hour later outside his house. Next morning a dead sheep was found washed up against the bank a little further down the river from where my friend had been fishing.

In reality, we know that such superstition may be unfounded as there is nothing about in the dark that wasn't there in the day – or is there? Standing there alone

A dark night on the River Lune.

in the dark the imagination starts to play cruel tricks: the knotted limbs of dead trees appear like the arms of some heinous witch ready to strangle you. The wind makes a strange haunting noise as it whistles through the rocks. Voles rustle in the grass by your feet. Bats and owls on silent wings fill the heart with trepidation. The clock in the haunted church tower higher up the valley strikes the midnight hour, the time for witches, warlocks, goblins, ghosts and all that is evil to be abroad. Was that mist rising or was it the ghost of the white lady? Was that a heron that glided overhead, or was it a vampire? The hairs on the back of your neck stand on end. You look about, straining your ears and eyes through the darkness. What am I doing here? And then an unfamiliar noise. You freeze. What was that? You wish you hadn't come.

I have spent my life in the country and have gained a great deal of knowledge about its nocturnal life, which can be fascinating. I know what sound each animal or bird makes and feel just as much at home in the dark as I do by day, but I have to admit that there was one occasion that scared the living daylights (or perhaps nightlights) out of me – an occasion I will never forget.

It was a very dark and drizzly night as I fished on the River Doon in Ayrshire. I had taken three sea trout in the early part of the night but now the fish had gone down and were proving difficult. It would have been about two o'clock when I heard a noise in the undergrowth some ten yards behind where I was standing. I ignored it, even though I was unsure what had made the noise. Probably a fox or a roe deer – I continued fishing. A few minutes later I heard the same unfamiliar noise again and was tempted to look round, but I resisted; to do so would be to admit that I was bothered. I wasn't scared of the dark, not me, never! I carried on fishing, but a few minutes later I heard another noise as something crunched the gravel behind me. Must be a roe. No, I would not look round. Don't be stupid Jim. I would not give in to fear. Hard case me, or so I tried to convince myself. I continued to cast, but a few moments later the gravel crunched again, this time a little closer. Of course I was feeling just a little concerned. What if it was someone out to rob me, or worse. I fought to control my growing dread. Who in their right mind would travel miles out into the country to rob the likes of me when there were easier pickings in the town. I was just being stupid. But what if it was some evil creature of the night. Something heavy had made that noise – a cloven hoof, the devil. What if? Stop it now, I told myself. You're a grown man.

This being the River Doon and close to Alloway, the home of Robert Burns, the thought of the bard's famous poem Tam O'Shanter suddenly came into my head. Tam had been drinking in the town of Ayr and, well under the influence, was making his way home on his old mare Maggie when he was chased by all manner of evil ghosts, warlocks and witches.

So Maggie runs, the witches follow,
Wi monie an eldritch skriech and hol-
low.

Tam's only chance of escape was to reach the keystone of the bridge over the river, as evil spirits are unable to cross running water.

Now, do thy speedy utmost, Meg
And win the key-stane of the brig;
There, at them thou thy tail may toss,
A running stream they dare na cross.

And then the gravel crunched again, right behind me this time. I turned and looked straight into the evil red eyes of Satan himself. I smelt the foul stench from his nostrils, his face almost touching mine. Never in my life had I known such fear. I ran into the water, hoping it was true that evil dare not cross the purifying running water.

Not daring to look round I battled my way through the fast current towards the opposite bank, which was high and covered in roots and brambles. But I was too scared to think about it. I grabbed the brambles, which tore deeply into my hands, and hauled myself up

A nice sea trout from the River Lune. (Courtesy of Arthur Oglesby.)

the bank. Was the devil still behind me or had I escaped. Oh God save me.

Still trembling, I dared to look back into the darkness. I saw nothing. Had I escaped or was the devil just playing some evil game. It was then that the moon came out from between the clouds and I saw my tormentor clearly. For as long as I live I will never forget the sight of that bloody donkey running across the field – probably more terrified than I was.

So if you are of a nervous disposition and are uneasy about fishing alone in the dark, take comfort, as I have it on good authority that you will be protected from all evil if you rub yourself down with a clove of garlic before you set out – not even anglers will come near you.

3 Tackle and Tips

Choosing the right tackle can be daunting. Every tackle shop and magazine will give you a different version of what you will require, and anglers will argue until the cows come home over what is the correct tackle for sea trout fishing. I do not intend to get too deeply involved in this argument. It is far better that I keep to the basics and give you some good tips that, for the most part, are for the benefit of the beginner.

Rods

It is, of course, important to choose the right rod, but where do you begin when the market is flooded with so-called sea trout rods? I suggest that you buy a rod not less than 10ft long, say a No 7–8 rating with a stiffish action that will not only cast a long line without too much effort but, more importantly, will be capable of lifting a fair length of line off the water and casting out again without false casting. This is important at night when you have just the right length of line out to reach close to the opposite bank. With one flick the line is lifted cleanly off the water then back again in one single action. My own favourite rod is a 10ft 6in, 7–8, which was designed for reservoir fishing but which serves me perfectly for most of my sea trout fishing. (There are some exceptions, however. For example, I have often fished small rivers, which were overhung with trees, when a shorter rod of 7ft and a No 6 line was much more useful.) If you know the tackle dealer well enough, it would be helpful if you could try out the rod just to see how much line it is capable of lifting. A good sea trout rod should be capable of lifting, at the very least, 15 metres of line off the water, or grass, when under test.

We accept that much of our sea trout fishing will be done in wild and rugged places at night and that rods will get a fair amount of hammering against rocks and overhanging trees, so try to avoid those very expensive rods with poser appeal where you only pay for the name and are almost too frightened to get it out of the velvet bag. Buy a middle of the range rod that, in most cases, works just as well as those expensive well-finished ones. But, more importantly, buy a rod that you feel comfortable with. A man and his rod should be something of a long-lasting love affair. You should understand its mood and capability and exactly what you can achieve with it. You should practise with it at every opportunity. Only then will you become an expert in its use.

Fly Lines

Your most used line will be a floating one. There are hundreds of different types available, but my advice is to buy a double-tapered line of a well-known make. The advantage of a double-tapered line, as opposed to say a weight forward, is that it will roll out and land more gently on the water and has less chance of frightening the fish. A floating line will also give you greater sensitivity when fishing. A weight forward line will cast a greater distance, but if you are not well practised at night fishing it can often land with a belly flop, which is something to be avoided, especially when a gentle approach is required on slower moving clear water. A double-tapered line can be much more forgiving. Even if you are something of an expert caster by day, you might find that your casting technique is different in the dark. The most common mistake made is the speeding up of the casting action. It can take some getting used to. My own preferred floating line for night fishing is a double-tapered No 7, although when fishing with larger lures I usually change up to a No 8, as the weight of a heavier line helps to power out a heavier lure. It makes sense to use a rod that is capable of casting the required line – in other words it would not be a good idea to attempt to cast a No 8 line with a rod that is designed only to deliver a No 6 line.

Never buy a dark-coloured floating line. Remember that there is no such thing as total darkness. Even on the darkest of nights, there will still be enough light in the sky to make the silhouette of a dark line appear like a barge rope to a fish looking up.

In addition to a floating line, I suggest you have in your armoury an intermediate, a sink tip, a medium, and a fast-sinking line to meet all eventualities. Again, I suggest that these lines should be double tapered for better presentation. I am quite sure

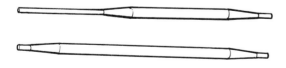

Figure 1. Fly line profiles. (Top) Weight forward line. The weight is concentrated at the end of the line, which allows for greater casting distance. (Bottom) Double-tapered line. The weight is concentrated in the belly of the line, which allows for a more delicate presentation.

that more experienced anglers will have no problem in presenting a weight forward line with a delicate touch, but I hope you will appreciate that many of the tips I give here are for the benefit of the beginner.

Backing Line

Your reel should be capable of holding at least 100 metres of backing line in addition to the actual fly line. To economise on backing line could prove costly as a big sea trout is capable of stripping a lot of line off the reel on the first run before it can be brought under control. I once hooked a large sea trout on the River Tweed at Coldstream, which took almost all of my 100 metres of backing before I was able to halt it. I personally prefer to use a braided nylon backing that, if for no other reason, being hollow cored is easier to attach to the fly line. If your reel is not capable of holding 100 metres of hollow, braided nylon backing, you should consider the alternative, which is to use the thinner terylene or similar material.

Again, for the benefit of the beginner, here are some simple instructions on joining the fly line to the braided backing line.

1   Once the backing line is wound onto the reel, thread the braided backing onto a darning needle. You will find this easier if you use a needle threader.
2   With the backing now threaded onto the darning needle, cut a piece of shrink wrap tube about ¾in long and thread this down the needle and onto the backing. Now remove the needle.
3   We will now need to push the end of the fly line inside the backing 'tube'. This is made easier by cutting the tip of the fly line to a point using a sharp craft knife or fly tying scissors. Now push the end of the fly line inside the

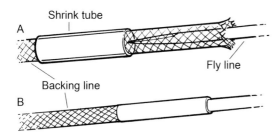

Figure 2. Joining the fly line to the backing line. See text for instructions.

distance of the cast by providing a greater transition of energy from the fly line to the fly and, consequently, a much better turnover and more gentle presentation is achieved.

In simple terms, a tapered braided leader is a length of braided nylon that is attached to the fly line at the thickest end. It then tapers down to the thin end on which is a small loop to which the leader, or tippit, is then tied. They are manufactured in floating, intermediate, sinking and fast sinking to suite a range of conditions and depths you wish to fish at. Some anglers like to use a sinking braided leader to a floating fly line in place of a sink tip line. Braided leaders are supplied in salmon or trout weights, but it is the trout weight that you will need.

A 'braided' leader should not be confused with a 'tapered' leader when making a purchase. A tapered leader is a length of nylon mono that tapers to a finer end. This is ideal for many forms of fly fishing, such as fishing a dry fly on a chalk stream for instance, but not an item I would personally include in my sea trout kit. Braided leaders are usually supplied in 5ft or 8ft lengths, although I prefer the 5ft length myself.

Attaching the braided leader to the fly line is done in much the same way as when

backing for a distance of about 1in (*see* Figure 2A). Pull the braided backing so that the mesh grips against the fly line, then glue over with flexible super glue. Note: Some manufacturers say that there is no need to use glue and that it is enough just to pull the backing tight before sliding the tube over the joint to maintain a hold. However, when fishing for sea trout I leave nothing to chance and prefer to use super glue.

4   Once the super glue has dried, slide the shrink tube down to cover the joint (Figure 2B). The tube will protect the joint from becoming damaged or frayed by the rod rings. Now hold the joint under a very hot tap or pour boiling water over it to shrink the tube. Do not tempt fate by using a cigarette lighter.

Braided Leaders and Braided Loops

At one time it was common to tie a knot on the end of a fly line, behind which the leader was attached. This, of course, made casting that much more difficult, as the knot interfered with the aerodynamics of the cast. A tapered braided leader makes the cast a much smoother one and increases the

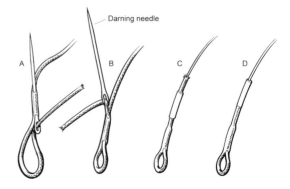

Figure 3. Assembling a leader loop. See text for instructions.

attaching the fly line to the backing. First the sleeve is threaded part way along the braided leader, then the end of the fly line is pushed inside the core of the braided leader. Super glue is then applied to the joint and when it has dried the shrink wrap is slid over the joint. As before, boiling water is poured over the joint to make the tube shrink.

An alternative to a tapered braided leader is a leader loop. Quite simply, this is a loop of braided nylon that fits to the end of the fly line, and to which the leader is attached. You can easily make your own braided loops from backing line (25–30lb B.S. is ideal). The method of attaching the loop to the fly line is exactly the same as with the tapered braided leader (*see* Figure 3).

Leader Material

There are so many makes that it would be an impossible task to recommend any particular one. New products, such as fluorocarbon, are virtually invisible in water and have a greater breaking strain in ratio to diameter. I personally never taper the cast but prefer to use 8lb breaking strain straight through. I never use anything less for sea trout simply because I would much prefer to land a fish rather than have one snap the leader with a hook still in its mouth. I would not want to go to bed with this on my mind. It also makes good sense to test all the knots carefully before beginning to fish.

I am often asked how long the leader should be. The best advice I can give is 2ft shorter than the rod you are using. For instance, if your rod is 10ft then the leader should be about 8ft long. If the leader is too long, and I know some that like to use a long leader, it would increase the chances of overcasting and getting the fly caught up on the opposite bank when night fishing. There are times, I admit, due to laziness,

when after changing the fly a few times the leader has become as short as 4ft yet I still continued to catch fish. But to allow the leader to become too short is not something I would recommend.

Flies and Fly Boxes

I will have much more to say about flies later on. The idea of sea trout fishing, particularly at night, is to keep things to a minimum. I know many sea trout anglers who will not venture out unless equipped with either a huge box full of flies, or perhaps half a dozen smaller boxes. There is little sense in this when it would be impossible to use so many different flies in the course of a night's fishing. One small box holding the essential patterns, which fits comfortably into your pocket, is surely enough. A box that will float if dropped into the water is preferred.

Reels

There are a vast list of reels available, but I recommend that you use a large arbour reel with a good drag system. This will eliminate tangles that frequently occur when line spreads and becomes tight against the housing. The drag, or clutch, if set correctly will help to tire a fish that is running hard and fast. A large arbour reel will also help to prevent lines from kinking and, in addition, you will be able to reel line in much faster on those occasions when you are playing a fish off the reel and it suddenly decides to run towards you – a frequent occurrence – which is why I personally use a larger 4in salmon size reel. Another tip is to choose a reel with fast-change spare spools.

Once again, I suggest that you buy a middle of the road priced reel. It wouldn't do to get a very expensive reel scratched or dented on the rocks in the middle of the night. Owning expensive tackle is very nice of course, but who's to see what tackle you are using in the middle of the night?

Landing Nets

Never use one of those landing nets with a collapsible frame. They will give you a lot of problems. For instance, they have a greater tendency to trail and become entangled in brambles and other types of undergrowth. I would also avoid those short-handled telescopic nets that are triggered by a spring. They are more trouble than they are worth. You should also avoid telescopic handles – you will not want to try extending one of these in the dark, or run the risk of the sections sliding apart when you are about to land that five pounder.

In most cases of sea trout fishing, the going will be tough, particularly if you need to wade in a boulder-strewn river. In these circumstances it is better to use a longer fixed-handle net of say 4ft long with a ridged frame – what I call a wading net. Mine is simply a course fishing handle with a 20in pan net. This type of net can serve two purposes, the obvious being as a landing net, but it can also serve as a wading staff. To prevent the handle from being pulled away by the current it should be weighted at the butt end, which is used to prod the river bed in front of you as you feel for hidden rocks and pot holes. Most handles of this type are hollow fibre-glass and have a screw-on cap, so the tip is to unscrew the cap and put about ten, 1oz lead (or lead substitute) round ledger weights (bullets) into the tube. The bullets can later be removed when not required.

Another tip for use with this type of net is to tape on a small torch about halfway along the handle. In those 'snaggy' situations when a fish runs under the bank, or between rocks or roots, you can then see exactly where the net is in relation to the fish by simply switching the torch on, although

shining a light into the water is something you should only do as a last resort, bearing in mind that doing so could ruin your sport for the next few hours, if not for the rest of the night. At least on that pool.

For fishing in less hazardous rivers, or where I know for certain that the bottom is snag free, I use a sea trout size gye net, which is slipped through the brass ring on my fishing bag, or the one attached to my belt.
Note: To comply with the law, all landing nets in the UK should be of knotless mesh to prevent unnecessary damage to fish.

Torches and Batteries

These are an essential part of any night fisherman's kit. I usually carry three torches. One is a headlight, the type that is similar to a miner's lamp except that the batteries are just two small ones that fit inside the lamp itself, not one of those heavy duty batteries that fit on a belt. This is useful when I want to change a fly. I also carry a good robust rubber torch, which will give me a good all-round and powerful light. This is the one I use when I get into one of those unexplained and frustrating tangles, which, thankfully, are not all that often these days. It is more often used for finding my way back to the car. The third torch is that mentioned under 'Landing Nets'. This is the one that is taped to the net handle: a tip I recommend when using a longer handled net. All torches should be the waterproof type.

Do make sure that the batteries you use are fully charged. Nothing can be more frustrating than trying to change a fly in poor light, or worse still, no light at all. It does no harm to carry a couple of spare batteries in a plastic bag.

Clothes

You should bear in mind that it can sometimes get very cold in the middle of the night, even if the day has been a scorcher. Long, warm summer nights are few and far between so it makes sense to take a warm jumper along, even if you don't use it. This might seem obvious, but how many times have you heard of so-called climbers being rescued from the mountains suffering from hypothermia, wearing inappropriate clothing?

Fishing waistcoats with countless pockets are something else to be avoided. Nothing can be more annoying than having to search through all those pockets for a spool of nylon, or some other small item.

Always wear a pair of thermal socks inside your waders. It is surprising how soon the feet get cold, especially when you are stood in water.

If you need to wade you should wear a short wading jacket and if you need to wade in deep water then you should consider wearing an inflatable jacket or collar. It goes without saying that great care should be taken when wading, particularly at night. If you are fishing alone you should let someone know where you are and your expected time of return. This applies to both day and night fishing.

Carrier Bag

As silly as it might seem, it is a good idea to take along a white carrier bag to put your catch in. It will save you the trouble of having to carry the extra weight around or having to wash out your fishing bag. Your catch can then be hung on a fence post or the branch of a tree out of the reach of predators and, being white, it can easily be found again.

Belt

A belt is another good idea and I don't mean to keep your pants up. Even if you are wearing a jacket it makes good sense to wear a good leather belt on the outside so that you can clip or hang your landing net or torch on it whilst you are fishing. Much better than trying to stick it down the leg of your waders!

Glasses

If you need glasses to chance a fly then do tie them round your neck. I've had a few pairs fall into the water and more than a few pairs left somewhere on the bank in the dark, either to be stood on or lost.

Insect Repellent

Never go without this. I have been eaten alive on too many occasions when I forgot to take some along. One of the most unforgettable experiences was when fishing on the River Add near Crinan. Scottish midges are some of the most ferocious you will ever encounter, with the Welsh variety coming a close second.

Priest

This is an item you should never be without. If you intend to kill a fish it should be done as humanely and quickly as possible. On too many occasions I have seen anglers leave fish floundering on the bank while they went in search of a stone to hit it with. Do not play into the hands of those who, through their own ignorance or political agenda, would have our sport banned.

Food and Drink

Don't take cold drinks on night fishing trips. Take a big flask of tea or coffee, or even soup. If you don't fancy eating sandwiches, at least take along some chocolate bars or cakes. These will give you energy to keep you going through the night. I might mention here my good friend Eddie Huyton, who is a keen sea fisherman. One cold winter night, Eddie drove the 80 plus miles from Warrington to Holyhead to fish for cod. As he was getting his tackle out of the boot of his car, disaster struck. His flask of coffee fell out of his bag and was smashed. Eddie did no more than put his tackle back in the boot and drove all the way home again. I think I would have done the same. My flask is my best companion on night excursions.

No doubt I could fill the rest of the pages allotted me on tips and tackle, but I feel that I have said enough on this subject. All I have to say here is keep it simple and travel light.

Old reels and new flies.

4   Dividing the Night

As described by the late Hugh Falcus in his book *Sea Trout Fishing*, night fishing in average summer conditions falls into four parts in much the same way as a game of football, these being: the first half, half time, the second half and extra time. I think it is a reasonably accurate guide to catching sea trout after dark, although I must stress here that not all nights will divide in this way. There will always be exceptions to the rule in sea trout fishing.

THE FIRST HALF

The river is now clear and at, or close to, its usual summer level. As the sun begins to sink, sea trout start to become active and make their presence known. First the odd plop as a fish hits the surface. Then as it gets a little darker more fish begin to show until eventually just about every sea trout in the river has a turn at showing off. Some will crash as if a large stone had been thrown in. Others will hit the surface and make an unmistakable fluttering sound as their tails rattle the surface. Sometimes they will be showing an interest in flies and insects of the natural kind and even when there is no obvious natural life on the surface this activity still takes place. Many fish will take advantage of the darkness to run upstream, leaving the pool you are fishing to be replaced by newly arrived fish, which are usually obliging and will often take the fly with relish, particularly if they are fresh up from salt water with their feeding instinct still in overdrive.

Dusk on the Cumbrian Esk.

Of course this is the ideal sea trout fishing scene, but on some rivers I have fished, particularly in South Wales, and I think of the Towy as one example, this kind of early surface activity does not always take place. Nevertheless the fish are just as likely to be caught in the first few hours of darkness as they would on any other river, but why this is so, I have no idea. The other exception is on hot and balmy nights when the temperature remains high all night long; nights when we don't need to wear a coat; the nights that are few and far between. On nights like these sea trout will usually be active at the surface all through the night.

In looking back through my fishing diaries I came across the notes I made in regard to a particular night in July when I fished on the River Teifi near Llandyssul; a night that is well worth a mention.

I had been looking forward to this trip as I hadn't fished with Lenny for some three years. He is an expert sea trout fisherman who has his finger on the pulse when it comes to sewin fishing on this river, and I was hoping that with his expert guidance I would get me a fish or two. It had seemed, however, that every tractor in Wales had been on the road that evening, causing me to creep and cuss, but eventually, over an hour after our agreed meeting time, I pulled into the paddock wondering if Lenny had given up on me. But there he was with his usual welcoming smile and the proverbial woodie stuck in the corner of his mouth.

In the dusk we walked along the river bank enjoying a good chin-wag while weighing up the water that, to me, seemed in perfect fettle with one exception. By now I had expected to see a few sea trout beginning to show but there was no sign of a fish, not even a minnow's dimple. Lenny said that it had been like this for the past few nights. No fish showing is very unusual on the Teifi in July, although, he assured me, there were plenty of fish in the river. The best tactic,

he advised, was to fish small fry imitations, just below the surface. There is nothing to equal local advice because he was right.

I chose to use a Tammy Troot as there is something about this fly that gives me confidence. The first pool I fished was about ten yards wide, with the deeper water on the opposite bank running at an easy medium pace. With Lenny still chatting away by my side – he had preferred to keep me company for the time being – I started at the neck of the pool and worked my way down, casting across at about forty-five degrees, a mend in the line that allowed the fly to hold nicely in the stream as it moved downwards until it was time to move a few paces down and cast again: easy classical fishing. Almost towards the end of the pool, where a pile of rocks forms a natural wall rising out of the river, I got that certain feeling that a good fish was waiting. And it was. Something told me to take more care about how I presented the fly at this point. A cast more gentle than before, a cautious mend of the line and a deep breath as the fly moved alongside the wall. I somehow knew that I would get a take, and I did – a hard solid take. The next thing a heavy fish was rushing about the pool. It put up a great scrap until Lenny eventually slipped the net under it, a beauty of 3lb.

We made our way down to the next pool where, for the next twenty minutes or so, I continued with Tammy Troot without any further success. Lenny suggested that it was probably a little too dark by now for this fly and that I should try something a little darker, something which would have a more pronounced silhouette. The Black Fry came to mind and was duly tied on. This immediately produced another take and a little later another good fish of about 2lb was landed.

By now, Lenny had decided that it was time for him to start fishing. His choice of fly was similar to my own, a Stoats Tail dressed much slimmer than the usual pattern and with eyes painted on to give it a small fry appearance. And what a fly that was. Lenny took six fish on it in the space of an hour and not one weighed under 2lb.

It turned out to be an unforgettable experience with plenty of fish caught, but not once did a sea trout break the surface. The exception to the rule if ever there was one and I think the lesson is not to be too concerned if you do not see fish showing in the pools.

Most of the time the sea trout will be seen showing off as the sun begins to go down and it can be hard to resist the temptation to take an early cast, pushing aside the fact that the darker it is the bolder sea trout become in taking the fly. I can think of one or two exceptions when I have broken the golden rule and here's a good example. On some of the Lancashire and Cumbrian streams that I frequent, in the months of August and September, fish that tend to run upstream after dark will often congregate at dusk near the head of the pool – not in the run, but in the slacker water to the edge of it. During this waiting period they will cruise about close to the surface, sometimes with their backs out of the water and often making short, fast bursts as if warming up for a sprint, which, in actual fact, they are. At this time, it can be very tempting to have a cast at them. But any cast at these fish needs to be made with considerable caution.

One evening as I was walking along the River Ribble near Sawley I stopped to watch sea trout that were gathering in this way. There must have been at least fifty fish getting ready to run, but it was only just dusk and I knew how easy it would have been to scatter them should I get the cast wrong or if they got a hint of my presence in any way. I decided that if I was going to have any chance at all then a different approach was called for. I tied on a small size 16

Bloody Butcher; some kind of sixth sense told me it was the right choice for the occasion. I then waded out into the fast water some distance above the shoal and made a shortish cast downstream. I then paid line off the reel, letting the current carry the fly until it reached the end of the run and swung gently round into the slacker water and over the fish. It was taken immediately by a three pounder, and what a fight it put up too. This was many years ago but I have repeated this manoeuvre in this situation on a number of occasions since, with a limited amount of success.

Once the fish decide to run, they will go like express trains and stop for nothing until they reach the sanctuary of the next pool. Your only chance of catching them will be when the rapid runs over a distance and they stop to rest for a moment or two by a large stone or some other obstacle. Otherwise it is best to wait for them to arrive in the pool. I have never had much success fishing fast rapids at night and, on reflection, it is probably as well to avoid them for safety reasons alone.

When the fish arrive at the next pool they will sometimes rest in the pool's tail, where they join other fish that have not run but have dropped back in the pool. Here you will be in with a good chance. Other runners will not hang about in the tail but will swim directly to the middle of the pool, and you will often see the V of their wake on the surface as they go.

Unlike salmon, which require a greater depth of water, sea trout will often be tempted to run in shallow water. On many occasions I have watched sea trout splashing through very shallow runs as they force their way upstream, and, even when there was barely a trickle, I have seen them skittering over the gravel on their sides.

This first half activity is an exciting time and the urge to begin fishing as soon as sea trout start to show will be compelling. The experienced sea trout angler will resist the temptation to start too soon. Such wild and timid creatures have amazing night vision and sense of self-preservation and I try, on most occasions, to resist. But there are, as always, a few exceptions to the rule, and fish can sometimes be tempted to take an early offering. But, more usually, the angler who is patient is the one who catches the most sea trout, and often the biggest one. In the majority of cases, this flurry of activity will last for two or three hours before the fish 'go down'. Why this should be is only a guess but I would reason that the fish's behaviour is related to barometric pressure, however slight the change may be, and its feeding pattern at sea where it feeds on sand eels, whitebait and other small fishes, which shoal close to the surface in the evening. In this most productive part of the night there will be no time to

have a chat on your mobile, eat your sandwiches or stop for a smoke; it is a time to fish with determination. All too soon this exciting time will end, the river will become still and the best of the fishing will be over. This is when most anglers pack up and head off home. You could be forgiven for thinking that all the action is over but I can assure you that it is not. There is often a lull in fishing during the period known as half time, which can last for anything up to an hour, or even a little longer, before sport can be resumed, albeit at a slower pace. But nevertheless sea trout can still be taken in what is called the second half – it is simply a matter of changing tactics.

The transition period between the first and second phase of the night is often the time when the temperature drops, causing a mist to form over the water's surface. The river shrouds itself in a blanket for the

Clouds are gathering and promising a good night's sea trout fishing on this north country stream.

night and I have heard it said that the mist is the very rising of the river's spirit. Some anglers claim that mist has an effect on the quality of the fishing and on a few occasions it might, but I have personally taken fish in the thickest of mists so don't let this prevent you from fishing.

The one thing that can affect sport, however, is a bright moon. I have fished on cloudless nights under a full moon when sea trout were bouncing all through the night and caught nothing. Such nights can drive you completely round the bend. I recall one night in particular when fishing on the River Lune. The moon was so bright that there was never a need to use a torch except to tie on a fly. The night had begun with conditions looking perfect. The river was low and full of fish. In fact, it had been a long time since I had seen the river quite so full. The surface was simply boiling with them, and it would continue boiling with them all night long. But almost within minutes of starting the clouds rolled away and the night became as dawn. Throughout the night I tried every fly and trick in the book, without so much as a fish coming close. To add to my frustration, they were even jumping right under my rod as if they were laughing at me. The night finally merged into morning as the moon shrank and faded from yellow to white and the sun's first rays began to flood over the fells. With a strong sense of dejection it was time to leave. The sea trout had mocked me.

I walked back along the river bank thinking about the number of times I had heard anglers say that it didn't matter whether they caught fish or not, it was the being there in the country, at one with nature and all that that mattered, but for the moment all that seemed like a load of tosh – a feeble excuse for catching nothing. Why go fishing in the first place? Why not take up rambling instead if the catching of fish means nothing. Would, for instance, a dedicated

mountain climber be prepared to simply sit on the balcony of some Muren hotel and stare up at the north face of the Eiger? No, of course he wouldn't, no matter how spectacular the scenery might be. He'd want to be up there with the other climbers. Would a keen yachtsman be happy just to sit drinking Pims in the harbour when the wind was fresh from the south? A daft question, I'm sure. I love the countryside as much as any man, but as an angler my prize was the catching of a fish and it had been denied.

Then my eyes lifted to the fells to see the climbing sun's reflections burst with a profusion of orange, pink, red and ochre across the rugged landscape. The surface of the river twinkled and danced in the kaleidoscope of colour. Birds began to sing their early chorus, heralding the dawn in a celebration of life. To never see these hills again, to wander amongst the lichened crags, the limestone outcrops, the peat moors and the green oak forest. To never hear the music of the wind or to watch the ever-changing colours of the seasons along the valley floor. Never to be startled by a roe deer as it darts across my path, or be thrilled to see an otter. To never again explore the estuary sands leading down to the sea where the incoming tide rattles the shingle along the shore. Never to gaze again in wonder at this creation and occasionally contemplate a greater power beyond the comprehension of a simple fisherman.

I was mindful of a little story I had once heard about an angler who was returning home one morning along the river bank after fishing through the night for early sea trout. He hadn't expected to see anyone about so early in the morning and as he approached the end of the meadow he was surprised to come across a kindly looking old man sitting on a tree stump by the gate. 'Good morning,' said the old man.

'Good morning,' returned the angler.

'Yes, it is indeed. Don't you think it's beautiful along this river bank,' he said, more in the way of a comment than a question.

'Aye, I suppose it is,' the angler replied.

The old man nodded his head and smiled. 'Tell me, do you ever feel the presence of your creator when you come fishing here?'

'Not me,' replied the angler, 'I don't believe in all that stuff – God and all that rubbish.'

With his chin resting on his hand, the old man seemed to ponder on what the angler had said.

'Sorry,' said the angler, 'I didn't mean to – well, you know – offend you.'

'It would take a lot more than that to offend me,' replied the old man with an amused smile, then after a pause, 'Would you care to indulge an old man?'

'In what way?'

'Just sit there on the bank.'

The angler sat. 'Now what?'

'I want you to sit quietly, close your eyes and describe to me what you hear and feel.'

The angler, thinking that he might as well humour the old man, closed his eyes and after a short time he said. 'I can hear

the sheep over in that far field making a bloody row.'

'Anything else?'

The angler thought about it for a while, then; 'I can hear the leaves rustling in the trees, and I can hear a blackbird singing in the bushes … I feel the breeze and the warmth of the sun on my face … I hear a collar dove cooing in the wood … I can hear the sound of a flock of geese in the distance … I can smell the wild garlic along the edge of the river. I can hear the ripple of the river tumbling over the stones and brown trout splashing in the pool.'

Slowly, as though waking from a dream, the angler opened his eyes to find that the old man was no longer there.

As I continued along the path I imagined a curtain raised to hide all this from sight and suppressing all the sounds of nature. Only the river in my view, to fish and only fish and nothing else – and to hook a monstrous fish on every cast. Was this what I wished for? No, perhaps not.

I have fished on nights when the moon was up and caught sea trout, but it was usually when the moon was hidden from time to time by passing clouds or there was good shade under trees. As far as catching sea trout was concerned, I would think twice about venturing forth under a full moon and a cloudless sky.

HALF TIME

Now the first half period is over and we have reached the half time interlude. A time to change to an intermediate or sinking line, or perhaps even a fast sinking line depending on the depth of the water. A time also to chance your fly to something bigger, such as a sunk lure, which will fish close to the bottom where the fish now lie. This is also a time to take a well-earned break; the night could be a long one. Enjoy a warm drink

An 8lb sea trout taken early in the night by Paul Hopwood using a Blue Beard.

A much appreciated catch.

and a bite to eat before you begin the second half of your night's fishing. But before starting, do make sure that you check your tackle, and in particular, your knots.

THE SECOND HALF

We are now well into the night and the sea trout are lying deep. This is the time to fish with heavier lures, such as a Terror or Demon, or the versatile Snake Fly, or flies tied on Waddington shanks that will get down to the fish. As I have explained in greater detail elsewhere, lures fished near the bottom should be fished slowly. At this time it is not impossible to hook a salmon; I have taken quite a number of salmon late into the night. So, if there are salmon about, do make sure that your landing net is big enough to handle one. Do not expect fishing to be as productive as it was in the early part of the night and don't lose heart thinking that you might be wasting your time. In my early sea trout fishing days I often used to imagine that I was flogging a dead horse and was sorely tempted to head for home but, more often than not, my patience was

rewarded. I can think of a number of times when the night turned cold or my arm and back started to ache, or when I just felt tired, and just when I thought of packing it all in I got a take, and more often than not it was from a big fish.

I once fished on the River Deveron with a friend I used to work with. The early part of the night had indeed been good and we had both caught a good number of sea trout up to 2lb or so. But after midnight the fish went down and the midgies came out in abundance, eating away at my face, neck and hands until, by around 3am, I had had enough. I packed in, leaving my good friend, who was determined to stick it out, to get on with it. When I saw him the next day, his face was swollen and covered in white lotion that he had used to ease the pain caused by the thousand bites he had received. But it had been worth it. Just after I had left he had hooked and landed a 4lb sea trout, followed by two more at 3lb. Every time I think about that night I wonder if I did right by leaving, midgies or no midgies.

Just one more last cast. Dawn on the River Ribble. Time to expect a big sea trout or even a salmon.

EXTRA TIME

Eventually, a little before the first glimmer of light begins to creep over the fells, sea trout will become more active once again. A time not to be missed. Some of my biggest fish have been taken in the run up to, and around, dawn. It is now the time to revert to a floating line using the same flies as you did in the first half.

Eventually, the early light begins to wash across the hills and the sea trout once more become shy and elusive and retire to their daytime haunts. On occasions when it has been a really dull dawning, with the threat of rain in the air, I have been lucky enough to fish into what you might call extra, extra time, which is also a good time to take a salmon or two. But we all need to sleep and the time has arrived for us mortal souls to head for home, to devour that bacon butty before crawling into a warm bed to dream about the next time.

5 Thoughts on Sea Trout Flies

The development of sea trout flies has come a long way in recent times. Early sea trout flies were no more than trout flies dressed on larger hooks. Some have proved deadly and have stood the test of time, earning their place in history. Famous flies, such as the Black Pennel, the Dunkeld, the Alexandra, the Bloody Butcher, the Mallard and Claret and the Peter Ross are but a few that spring to mind. Many bare no resemblance to a living creature, having been tied as no more than a whim by their creator, yet nevertheless they catch fish. Then came such flies as the Medicine, invented by Hugh Falcus. This fly, with its slim profile and silver body, was to prove one of the deadliest sea trout flies of all time. It is a fly that will take fish by day or by night and in almost any conditions. With it came flies such as the Secret Weapon, with a trailing treble behind a leading hook on which a maggot or two can be fixed to combat those fish that, on occasions, prefer to tweak at the fly rather than take with gusto. Even without maggots, this is still a great lure. So too, the wake lure became popular, a deadly method of catching sea trout. Hair-wing flies also became popular as the 20th century progressed. They were less stiff and consequently more life-like than the traditional patterns, and it wasn't long before fly-dressers were tying up hair-wing variations of the tried and tested feather-winged traditionals. Waddington shanks and tube flies also came into fashion, being ideal for hair wings.

It now seems that we have moved into the glitter-bug age. Flies that incorporate flashy strands of fine tinsel in every colour under the sun are now in vogue. Holographic, fluorescent, luminous and phosphorescent materials that glow in the dark have also gained in popularity. Hair wings will sometimes have a few strands of tinsel mixed in or be made entirely of tinsel. In a good many lures, bodies are now of bright iridescent tubing and are extremely attractive both to fish and anglers. Without doubt such materials deserve their place in the modern fly fisher's armoury; they have certainly made a difference to fish catches.

Many people believe that, like salmon, sea trout cease to feed once they enter the river. Personally, I am unable to go along with this theory as I have often caught sea trout that had the remains of small fish,

Two tube flies (top and middle) and a Snake Fly (bottom).

41

crustaceans, and various insects in their stomachs. They do feed in fresh water but at a lower intensity than they might at sea. However, the longer a sea trout remains in fresh water the less it is inclined to feed as its body adapts from a sea- to a freshwater environment. When the river is up and coloured you can catch sea trout with considerable ease on worms, maggots or other live bait, and even on fly or spinner for that matter. However, in normal summer conditions, by which I mean when the river is low and clear, or at least running towards clear, they might not be so obliging. But they can still be tempted to take a well-presented fly, particularly after dark. It might, therefore, be interesting to ponder for a while on the reasons why a fly should be taken and why some flies are likely to work better than others.

It is generally accepted that there are three reasons why a migratory fish will take a fly. These are: curiosity, aggression and the instinct to feed. So we now need to ask which of the three instincts is any particular fly likely to trigger. Let us suppose, for instance, flies with a silvery body are taken as small fish. If this is the case then it is worth considering that on their journey along the coast sea trout feed mainly at dusk and into the first few hours of darkness on sand eels, whitebait, and other small fish that shoal near the surface. This is possibly why the early part of the night is the most productive. Consequently, it could be reasonably argued that this is why a silvery fly fished high on a floating or intermediate line at this time is likely to be more successful than others. We can now take a calculated guess that such a fly triggers off the feeding instinct.

If there are moths or sedges etc. on the water's surface in the early part of the night, the chances are that sea trout will be showing an interest. I have watched them slashing away at such on countless occasions and

a few moths will almost certainly be eaten, although this cannot be described as any kind of feeding frenzy otherwise the fish would be easy to catch. More often than not, the sea trout are simply examining whatever is causing the disturbance. Perhaps this is the curiosity factor rather than a feeding instinct, as moths and sedges form no part of a sea trout's diet at sea. Unlike ourselves, a fish is unable to hold things in its hand for closer inspection; it can only use its eyes and mouth, which, in fact, it does and at a speed that is almost beyond conception.

I believe that the main reason why a larger lure fished deep in the middle of the night is attacked is because it invades the seat trout's space. The Terror or similar type of lure works well in the 'second half' and the slower it is fished the better it will work. A lure fished quickly through the pool will have little success because the sea trout thinks it is just another fish passing by and in its lethargic state it will have no inclination to chase after it. But a lure fished dead slow is likely to make a sea trout think that another fish is about to take up residence in its own allotted space and it consequently attacks it. The sea trout is further aggravated by having its state of semi-sleep disturbed by an invader. A lure will also be attacked when fished too near the redd of a spawning fish.

Even the most ridiculous looking fly, if presented well and fished in a manner that gives it some resemblance of life, will catch a sea trout or two from time to time, but flies designed with a little more purpose will account for more fish. We would do well to remember that a sea trout has a greater sense of self-preservation than any other creature on the planet. He is the ultimate hunter and master of his realm; any fly dressed to tempt him should be one that attempts to send all his senses into overdrive. Let's take a look at the

Medicine as a good example. This highly successful fly, which has a slim silver body, a few turns of hackle at the throat and a slip of bronze mallard or black and white striped teal for a wing is obviously imitating a small fish. Few fish, however, are so slim as a Medicine, except (you've probably guessed already) an eel. A small eel. What about a sand eel? This would make sense as sand eels, *Ammodytes tobianus*, the most common inshore variety, form a large part of the sea trout's sea diet. So we now see the picture beginning to emerge. The Medicine is more likely than not triggering a feeding instinct. However, the Medicine is not dressed to look exactly like a sand eel, only a hint of one, so there may be a case to argue that this fly not only sparks the feeding instinct but also the fish's curiosity, thus doubling its catching potential. Let's develop this a little further.

If you were to study a picture of a sand eel the chances are that the most noticeable part would be its eyes. A dot on an otherwise white background. So I ask myself if sand eels (and other fishes) are recognised by their eyes and does the addition of eyes play a part in further convincing the sea trout of the lure's credibility. I am sure the answer is yes. I can give you many examples of times when Medicines, and other fish-representing patterns that I have added eyes to, have worked with remarkable results.

To illustrate this point, I travelled with my old friend, Bill Thompson, one evening to fish on the River Derwent in Cumbria. We had discussed my theory of eyes on the way there, so just for the hell of it, Bill suggested we carry out an experiment. For the first hour we both fished with Medicines, except mine had eyes. In this period I took four fish to Bill's one. We then changed over and I fished a Medicine without eyes and vice versa. Over the next hour I caught nothing while my good friend took five.

I appreciate that by no means could this be said to be a scientific experiment, still, I think it adds a little weight to the argument.

Another example is my Uncle Wullie's variation of the Alexandra, an excellent pattern on which I caught my very first sea trout. His was dressed much slimmer than the original pattern and possibly looked more like a small fish, which, in my opinion, is the reason it worked so well. In later years I added eyes to it and have now lost count of the number of fish it has taken.

Progressing from here, I took the sand eel imitation a stage further and in 1985 the Snake Fly was born. What I set out to achieve was a lure that not only looked like the real thing but had a flexible body that gave it 'action'. It wasn't meant to be called a Snake Fly. It was when I showed the pattern to my old fishing buddy, Howard Heaton, that he declared that it looked like a bloody snake; and so the name stuck. This too will take even more sea trout when eyes are painted on it. I could also add here that many of the more successful flies for sea trout, and salmon, are dressed with jungle cock feathers – some anglers swear by them. However, I do not believe that jungle cock (the eyed cape feathers) have any particular magical properties, except that they are highly fluorescent when held under an ultra-violet light. I am inclined to believe that the reason why they often work so well is that they are simply taken as eyes, although they do make an attractive fly.

There are times when sea trout take the fly with relish and equally there are times when they simply tweak away and all the angler feels is the tap, tap, tap of a fish that is playing with the fly – a frustrating and frequent occurrence when rain or thunder is due or when the temperature drops. Consequently, unlike salmon flies, which are often dressed to represent shrimps or prawns and have fibres trailing far beyond

The exception to the rule. This fine sea trout was taken on a Curry's Shrimp Fly.

the hook to appear like feelers, a good sea trout fly should be dressed, as far as possible, within the bounds of the hook; in other words such trailing bits on a sea trout fly is not encouraged as, almost certainly, these are the bits that a sea trout will all too often nip at while missing the hook entirely. The Secret Weapon and the short-dressed fly range, which we will deal with later, serves to hook any short-taking fish. However, the general rule should apply to all sea trout fly dressings. I can think of a few exceptions, but the first that springs to mind is the Haslam. This excellent fly has horns that extend beyond the hook and can be so

attractive to sea trout that breaking the rule can easily be forgiven.

So the development and search for the perfect fly goes on. And why not? This is what makes fly fishing so interesting and exciting. I have said that there is no need to carry a great box full of flies to the riverside and that you should travel light, but this does not mean that you should only dress the odd fly or two; you should try to dress new flies and fish them with every opportunity. This way we discover new things – we progress and share our ideas with our fellow fishermen. We should forever continue to be innovative, to experiment and to search for answers – there is so much yet to be discovered. We are, and always will be, the alchemists of fur, feather and tinsel. This is what drives us, what makes us tick.

I don't fish still waters for stocked fish all that often and I don't pretend to be any kind of expert on the subject, but what I have noted over the years on the subject of still-water flies is the stubborn belief in particular patterns. Not all, but many anglers will insist that if you go to such and such a water it would be a waste of time going without such and such a fly. There is one northern reservoir that I occasionally fish to lessen the withdrawal symptoms when waiting for the sea trout season to begin. I am always told that the best pattern for this water is a Viva, and without doubt it catches more fish than any other. Most anglers fishing there will swear by it. The 'must have it' theory probably started after someone had a great day on it or caught the record rainbow that was only stocked that morning; the angling press said 'caught on a Viva', and before you know where you are everyone's using them. But what they don't seem to realise is that so many fish are caught on it, not because it is such a fantastic fly, but because hardly any other fly is used there.

A lesson from the past. This lure, which dates back to about 1920, is made from canvas that is shaped over a 'Terror' mount and sewn on the underside. This one, with a flat profile, swims with a fluttering action that gives the appearance of a wounded fish. Something the modern fly-dresser might like to improve upon.

So there's the obvious answer.

When it comes to fishing for sea trout, however, anglers do not congregate in numbers or spend time chatting in the lakeside shop. In fact, they only meet up with one another on rare occasions. Their confidence in any particular fly is not one borne of rumour or gossip or accounts of big fish catches in the angling press. It is usually a confidence based on trial and error over a long period. Such are the flies that I have described in this book. Some are my own inventions while some are the creations of others whose help and generosity over the years has been of enormous value. They are the flies that I personally have confidence in, based on a lifetime of experience and experimenting. They are the flies that I hope you too will have confidence in after reading my book. I will give you the patterns so that you can have a go at tying them for yourself – there is nothing so rewarding as catching a fish on a fly of your own tying.

6 Small Fry

In this chapter I will describe some highly successful patterns that are designed to represent small fish and sand eels. Some are relatively easy to dress and even if you have never tied flies before you should soon get the hang of it with a little practice. Where the dressings are more complicated I have gone into a little more detail and hope that you will be able to follow my instructions without too much difficulty. Under this heading I had no difficulty in choosing the fly to begin with, which is:

REUBEN'S SPECIAL
(A Gypsy's secret)

I am thinking about a time when I fished on the River Clwyd in North Wales, a river that, at the time, I was not too familiar with. It was a perfect fishing night at the end of August – dark and overcast with the river running low and clear. I had walked the beat earlier but had not seen any fish about. Perhaps they were lying in the deeper holes from which they would later emerge once the sun went down. I was still hopeful.

In such ideal conditions I often start with smaller flies dressed on a size 10 single and sometimes a size 12 double or even a small treble. I often used to fish a dropper in my earlier fishing years but seldom bother these days; it all seems too much trouble. Not only that, I have often fished with friends who were fishing droppers and still caught just as many, if not more fish on some occasions than they did. If you think

your chances are doubled by using a dropper then by all means try it, but remember that your chances of a line tangle are increased ten-fold and there is nothing so frustrating as trying to sort the mess out in the dark. My tip, as always, is to keep things simple.

As it became dusk I was hoping that the sea trout would begin to show, but none did and my hopes of success began to fade. Perhaps the cool breeze, which had got up, was keeping them down, but I doubted it. Perhaps there just weren't any fish in the beat or perhaps they had run through to the Junction Pool above on the last tide. I couldn't afford to fish there anyhow. Still, I was here now so I would have to give it my best shot.

I worked my way with stealth down through those beautiful pools and runs, hoping that maybe an odd big fish might

A beautiful sea trout taken on a small fry imitation dressed with holographic materials which reflect more light.

still be lurking, but I never even got so much as a pluck from one of the cheeky little brownies that abound on the lower Clwyd. I fished on until I had exhausted every trick in the book. Nothing. I then remembered that the tide which causes the level of the pools on this lower beat to back up was due in about another hour; perhaps a fresh run of fish would arrive with it. In the meantime, I would return to the car and enjoy a coffee while I waited.

As I neared the car, I noticed that another car was parked next to mine and that two anglers were obviously intent on fishing. We soon struck up a lively conversation. These were knowledgeable and likeable local characters who knew the river well. They were Bob Deed and Geraint Roberts. They too were waiting for the arrival of the tide.

As the two began to tackle up I couldn't help noticing that Geraint's right hand was a mechanical one, yet, to my admiration, he continued to put his rod up without effort. I also noticed that his rod handle had been specially adapted.

As the tide began to push up and raise the level of the Barrier Pool a few inches or so, Bob and Geraint began to fish. I know the difference between good and less than good fly fishermen and it was apparent that these two were experts. Geraint's handicap had no effect on his casting ability, or his catching ability for that matter. He was soon into a reasonable fish, and a few minutes later Bob too had taken a nice fish. This gave me renewed enthusiasm so I set off back down the river at a pace. I needn't have bothered – I still caught nothing.

The following week I met up with my two new friends once more and wasted no time in asking them what they had taken their fish on. 'Talk to him,' said Bob, 'He's the expert.' The fly that Geraint then gave me, and which, remarkably, he had tied himself, was like no other I had ever seen or heard of

before. It was, I was told, a Reuben's Special. I was intrigued. It is a lure to represent a small fish and works particularly well in estuaries and lower river beats where fresh run fish can be expected. I have since used this fly on a number of other rivers with remarkable success.

Geraint told me the history of the fly and something about himself, which is well worth relating.

Geraint is descended from a long line of Romany Gypsies who once travelled all over Wales making a slender living by playing the harp for the gentry – and even royalty. Geraint's great-grandfather, Reuben, once played for Queen Victoria. He also played at the official opening of Lake Vyrnwy, where he worked as a keeper for some time.

Reuben's brother, Lloyd Wynn, born in 1844 at Llanuwchllyn, was also an exponent of the Welsh triple harp and a great angler too. It was he who invented the Penybont, a superb fly for trout and sea trout that is still fancied locally to this day.

In addition to being a fine harpist, Reuben, like his brother, was also a famous fly-dresser and his work was much in demand. One fly that Reuben invented was so deadly that the secret was kept within the family for generations. Only Reuben's descendants knew the magic formula – until now that is.

In 1966, at the age of seven, when Geraint already knew a thing or two about fishing, he would occasionally go down to the local village butcher's shop to earn some pocket money by helping out with the sausage making. The butcher had warned him not to let any bones drop into the mixing machine but accidents happen and sure enough some bones ended up in the mixer. Geraint tried to pull them out but it was no use, his hand was minced along with the pork.

Geraint is a philosophical kind of guy and I couldn't help but chuckle when he remarked that such was the true meaning

Geraint Roberts fishing the Castle Beat on the River Clwyd in North Wales.

The original Reuben's Special. Over the years this unorthodox fly has taken countless sea trout on the River Clwyd and other Welsh rivers. This one has accounted for dozens of sea trout, hence its chewed up appearance.

of lending a hand. The Gypsy's secret is hereby revealed.

The dressing here is the original one as dressed by Reuben himself. The materials you will need are:

A size 10 long shank hook
Fine pale yellow wool
Foil from a cigarette packet or a wine bottle
Peacock herl
Pale yellow tying silk

Construction

1   Place the hook in the vice and wind on a bed of the silk from the eye to the bend and catch in the yellow wool.
2   Wind the wool up to the eye, tie in and snip off the excess.
3   Cut a strip from the foil and tie it in a little way up from the bend. Now wind it on until it is just a little short of the eye.
4   Take a few strands of the peacock herl, tie them in behind the eye, and again at the bend. Now snip off the excess at both ends leaving a short stubby tail.
5   Make a few tight turns of the silk behind the eye just to secure things then apply a drop of varnish.

You may think this is something of an unrefined dressing but bear in mind that in those days fly-tying materials were not so easily come by. Moreover, it seems to matter little that this fly does not conform to modern tying methods – it is a killer. If you want it to fish near the surface then cigarette packet foil is fine, but if you wish it to carry a little more weight then wine bottle foil will do the trick, although I would be inclined to apply some varnish over it before use.

Over the years the pattern has changed slightly. Geraint's friend Bob uses a slightly different variation of the dressing, which works wonders. Here it is:

Bob Deed's dressing

Hook	Size 10–4 long shank
Silk	Yellow
Body	Dressed to end slightly round the hook's bend. First a tag of fluorescent wool, then silver tinsel, then another short part of the wool just behind the eye
Wing	This is not a wing as we know it but strands of peacock herl tied down over the body as with the original
Head	Yellow

Bob has sometimes made the tag of just the tying silk, which he has painted over with luminous paint.

BLACK FRY

This is a great fly to use on a dark night, particularly in the first two hours or so – the 'first half'. It can also be good in the day when the river is still a little stained and running off. I gave some of these flies to my friend Dave Pritchard, who has made some remarkable catches on it, such as his best ever sea trout, a 6lb grilse, and a baseball cap.

There is an ancient stone bridge that crosses a certain stream in Wales, which I fish from time to time. The pool below this bridge is known, surprisingly enough, as the Bridge Pool, and an excellent pool it is too, but if I had my way I would change the name of it to Dave's Pool. Dave, who fishes here as often as his wife will allow him, is a great believer in the Black Fry because it was in this very pool that he caught his best ever sea trout on this fly, which I dressed for him. Although it was a

beautiful fish of 10lb, it will not be his fine fish that I will remember the pool for, but for an ugly, yet funny, incident that took place there.

There was still some colour in the water from a good downpour the previous day, so Dave and I decided that some daylight fishing might still be productive before the river cleared, which in this stream would not take long. We met by the bridge and, knowing how much he loves to fish the Bridge Pool, I went to fish the next pool down.

It would have been about 3pm when I noticed a youth of about seventeen, wearing a baseball cap, standing on the bridge. There was something about this youth that gave me a twinge of uneasiness. I kept him in view for a while through the corner of my eye, but after about ten minutes or so my concentration drifted away from the boy and back to my fishing. That's when I heard the loud splash.

I immediately looked towards Dave, thinking he must have hooked a good fish, but this was not the case. The youth had tossed a boulder off the bridge. Dave was furiously shaking his fist at the idiot, who seemed to think it was funny and began to make two-fingered gestures. My friend, who is a hard ex-slate miner, is not the man to stick two fingers up at, let alone have his fishing ruined. He threw down his rod and ran towards the bridge with the obvious intention of giving the youth a thick ear. But at the age of fifty something the chances of catching him were not good. The youth took off like a greyhound.

After a cup of coffee, a cigarette and some consoling words from myself, Dave managed to get his temper under control and resumed fishing once more under the bridge. It seemed that the youth's boulder had not put the fish down, but had rather woken them up. He was soon into a heavy fish that, from the way it bolted upstream under the bridge, looked more like a salmon than a sea trout. And it was. After a great scrap I put the net under his fish, a lovely fresh sea-liced grilse of about 6lb. As my friend remarked how the youth might have done him a favour I looked up towards the bridge. The youth was back. I could see his intention and tried to warn Dave. But it was too late. The youth hurled a large stone, which struck him with a thud behind his left ear.

I am not saying that what happened next was a good or a bad idea or how dangerous such an act might have been, but wounded and with blood running down his neck, Dave was raging mad. He cast straight at the youth. The fly caught into his baseball cap, which was yanked clean off his head. I'm not sure if this is what Dave had intended but if it was then it had to have been the most brilliant cast I had ever seen. The youth was now screaming that he wanted his baseball cap back. Dave told him to come and get it. With that, the boy made his way down the path by the side of the bridge carrying a stone the size of an ostrich egg.

Now the two sized each other up. The youth threatened to let fly with the stone, while Dave, rod poised at ten past, threatened to whip out the line like a bullwhip. They circled each other. The cap in the ring. Who would make the first move? Who would be the fastest draw? Thoughts of Garry Cooper in High Noon flashed through my mind.

As the standoff continued, a police car drew up and two officers got out. They stood on the bridge watching the strange goings on with disbelief until, at length, one of the officers called 'Hey you'. The youth looked up, dropped his weapon and ran hell for leather across the fields, clearing a number of fences like an Olympic hurdler.

The policemen offered to take Dave to the hospital, especially as it looked as though he might require a couple of stitches, but Dave had no intention of wasting any more fishing time and settled for a big plaster from the police first-aid box.

The dressing

Hook	Size 10 Partridge Single Wilson (or Michael Frodin)
Silk	Black
Body	Flat silver
Rib	Fine oval silver
Hackle	Black cock hackle tied in as a false beard beneath and at the sides
Wing	Three or four holographic silver fibres with black cock hackle fibres over
Head	Black with white eyes

Note: The cock hackle fibres used for the wing are the longer fibres from the base of the same hackle that was tied in at the throat; the part that many fly dressers throw away. These longer fibres make excellent winging material as they are very flexible and life-like, especially in slower moving water.

The following two patterns also make good use of hackle fibres to form the wings.

BLUE BEARD

This is a similar fly to the Black Fry, and again one that works well in the early part of the night. I have often heard it said that sea trout are fond of the colour blue and I think there may be some occasions when a fly with a little blue in it will work when others fail. And a handsome fly it is too.

The dressing

Hook	Size 4–10 Partridge Single Wilson (or Michael Frodin)

Body	Flat silver, plain or holographic
Hackle	Blue cock fibres tied in false at the throat
Wing	Blue hackle fibres (the shade known to fly-dressers as 'teal' blue) with a few strands of pearl Krystal Flash mixed in
Head	Black with white eyes and red pupils

KERRY GOLD

This name has nothing to do with a well-known brand of butter. It got its name from a time when I once visited the beautiful Ring of Kerry in the west of Ireland.

I had made some enquiries at the hotel about the local fishing and was told that I should go to see a certain old gentleman who could be found at the hostel that he kept a few miles down the road.

On arriving at the hostel I was met by a large sign, not untypical in Ireland, which read: Hostel. Undertaker. Florist. Cobbler. Fishing Permits. An old lady came to the door and I asked her if the man was about. She said that she hadn't seen him for a while and suggested that I go look for him down the garden. I did, but there was no sign of him so I made my way back up the steep garden. Just then I heard a voice from above. 'Is it me you're wanting?' I looked up to see an old man with a mop of silver hair peering down at me from the roof. I told him I was looking for some good fishing. 'Wait there,' he called and proceeded to climb down a long ladder, so riddled with woodworm that it looked as if it was about to fall apart at any moment. But eventually he made it to the ground and led me into a shed at the side of the house. It was a fly-fisherman's Aladdin's cave with shelf upon shelf of fly-dressing materials and countless boxes of flies for every occasion. Most definitely a man of many talents.

I was soon sold a permit to fish the River Caragh, which flows from that most beautiful of lakes by the same name. He told

The author landing a nice sea trout on the River Caragh, Co Kerry.

51

me that a gold fly might work well at this time of the year (August), so to be polite I purchased three or four gold flies that the old man had tied himself and which he said were called Kerry Gold. They had orange hackle points as wings, which I changed for hackle fibres a few years later. His dressing, however, was nevertheless a useful one on which I caught a number of sea trout during that particular stay. I was now ready and eager to fish the river I had heard so much about, but it would be a little while yet before I was to have that privilege.

My wife, Heather, who had joined me on the trip, was keen to see Lake Caragh, having heard so much about how beautiful it was. No point in arguing, so I agreed to take her along. But as we neared the shore the road turned away from the lake and lead up the mountain. I followed it as it became narrower and steeper and I knew from the compass in my head that we were heading away from the lake. I thought about turning the car round but there was no room at the side of the boulder-strewn road, or track as it was by now, and besides there was a steep fall down the mountain if I got it wrong. Up and up we travelled, not knowing where the track would lead, but after a while we arrived at a T-junction. This was where things became even more frustrating: on a road sign an arrow pointed to the left and read Lake Caragh. The arrow pointing to the right also read Lake Caragh. This could only happen in Ireland. I chose to go right.

Now I was heading down the mountain. But with huge rocks, birch and broom on either side of the road I was unable to see if we were any nearer to the lake. So I pulled into the side and climbed to the top of an outcrop of rocks. As I stood there trying to look through the trees I heard a noise getting closer, put-put, put-put, put-put. Round the bend came a man on a clapped-out scooter; a crazy-looking character in

his forties with a wild mop of red hair. He stopped, leaned the scooter against a rock and walked towards me, almost tripping over the hem of his trench coat, which was so long that it trailed on the ground. Then, with a gormless smile that did nothing to conceal a row of protruding, bad, top teeth, he asked, 'Would you be lost?'

I asked him if he could tell me the way to the lake.

'Well,' he said, pointing up the mountain, 'some go that way'. Then he pointed down the mountain. 'And some go that way.'

I sighed, got back in the car and continued on my way.

After another mile or so and with the lake still not in sight, I again got out and climbed to the top of another rocky outcrop, but all I could see was still more trees. Then the put-put, put-put, put-put … The hairy man had caught up with me. 'Are y'still lost?'

'No, I'm just thinking of throwing myself down the bloody mountain.'

'Well it's a nice day for it, so it is.'

I got back in the car and drove on. Heather could see the funny side of it but I wasn't in the mood and continued downward wondering if I would manage to fish at all that day. However, things brightened up when I eventually arrived at the bottom of the mountain where the shimmering lake stretched out before me. Lake Caragh is, as far as I am informed, the only 'lake' in Ireland.

How beautiful Lake Caragh was. The colours of the forest and hills reflected on the water in a way that no artist could ever have captured on canvas. I remembered my old proof-reader, Phil Harris, who is now reading for the angels, telling me how he had been moved to tears the first time he had seen this wondrous place, and I could well understand how. I just had to take some photographs, so I got out the camera, tripod, and the rest of the gear and set it all up. Now I was ready to take some fantastic shots. And then put-put, put-put, put-put... Oh no. Not him again.

The mad man jumped in front of the camera. 'D' y'want to take me picture. Go on, all the Yanks take me picture. I'm famous back in the States, so I am.' He posed to the left. 'How about this way?' He posed to the right, 'Or this way?' I asked him politely to go away. 'Or this way.'

'I'm not an American. Please go away.'

He stood on a stone wall. 'How about this way then?'

'Just clear off. I'm trying to photograph the lake, not you.'

'How about this way then?'

All this time, Heather sat in the car obliviously reading her Ian Rankin. I moved the camera. The wild man jumped in front of it. 'Go on, go on. Take me picture. Don't you think I'm a good-looking fellow. I could have been a film star, so I could.'

As this performance continued I was finding it hard to contain my growing frustration. Eventually, I became so annoyed that I decided the best thing to do was to take his picture in the hope that he would go away. But he didn't. On and on he went. 'What about from this side? Don't you think I've got a nice head of hair?'

I'd had enough. I bundled the camera gear into the boot, slammed the lid shut, got in the car and felt in my pocket for the keys. They weren't there. I searched through my other pockets. No sign of them. I asked Heather if she had them. She looked up from her novel. Not me, she shrugged, then returned to Inspector Rebus. I got out and searched about on the ground.

'Have y'lost your keys then?'

'Go away!'

There was no sign of them. There was only one place they could be. In my state of irritation I had thrown them into the boot along with the photographic gear. The man stood there grinning as if it were all a bit of fun. I just had to get away before the man drove me insane. I also needed to open the boot. Nothing for it; like a man possessed I wrenched out the back seat, which I threw on the grass. The wild man sat on it. 'Just like a picnic this. Have y'got anything to eat? I could just murder a chicken leg, or what about a nice pie – I like pies.'

'Sod off!' He ignored me.

Through the hole behind where the seat had been I began to fish out the boot's contents. First my fishing jacket, then my fishing bag, a sweaty pair of thermal socks, then the camera bag, then the tripod, then more items of loose fishing tackle, including a fly that stuck in the back of my hand. And then, at last, the keys.

I quickly opened the boot and chucked everything back inside. Next I dragged the seat from under the mad man's flea-ridden trench coat and threw that inside the car. 'Are y'sure y'don't want to take another picture of me before you go.'

'Just shut up.'

I put the key in the ignition. Please start. It did, and I drove away with the sight of the idiot waving in my rear view mirror.

I had driven a mile or so down the road when Heather looked calmly up from her book. 'I've just thought of something,' she said.

'What's that?'

'Well,' she said, with a sigh, 'If you wanted to open the boot, why didn't you just pull that lever under the dash.'

I make no further comment.

The dressing

Hook	Size 6–1/0 Kamasan B180 low-water salmon
Silk	Black
Body	Flat gold
Rib	Fine copper or gold wire
Hackle	Bright orange cock hackle fibres tied in false at the throat

A quiet pool on the River Hodder where sea trout lie under cover of the overhanging bushes. A perfect place to fish a small fry imitation in the early part of the night.

Wing	Bright orange cock hackle fibres same as the hackle
Head	Black with yellow eyes and black pupils

THE MEDICINE

Much has been written in the past about this fly and I am sure that much will be written in the future. This variation of the Blue and Silver, which was designed to represent a sand eel, was devised by the late Hugh Falcus and is probably one of the most successful sea trout flies ever.

I have used this fly extensively over the years and have caught scores of fish on it, particularly in the early part of the night when the sea trout are most active. It should be dressed on larger, fine wire hooks and the low-water Single Wilson is my first choice. You should not be afraid to dress this fly on larger hooks – a size 1 or even 1/0 is not too big. In summer conditions, I usually fish the Medicine close to the surface using a floating line. But on larger waters, when I want the fly to fish slightly deeper, I some-

times use an intermediate or sink tip line.

There is a stretch of day ticket water I sometimes fish on the River Ribble just above Ribchester, where the river is big and wide. This is not the easiest of waters to fish as it is difficult to get over the best lies due to the rocky outcrops that can make wading difficult. I often wish I owned this water; if I did I would invest in a little construction, which would, I'm sure, improve the access and the fishing no end. The river here leaves a giant of a pool at a deep and wide bend as it enters the start of this beat. Here the river picks up speed and runs behind a gravel island, which I sometimes fish from if the river is low enough to allow me to wade across to it, otherwise getting to it can be difficult and dangerous. I don't know why I bother trying to get to this island, but it looks 'fishy' and I like the way the fast current works the fly. However, I have caught very few sea trout in this fast run. It seems that once they enter it they go like bullets until they reach the great pool above. I have, however, caught plenty of good chub in it and once caught a barbel of 8lb.

From the island, the current continues at a fair speed under the far bank until it

The author fishing on the Cumbrian Esk, the home of the 'Medicine'.

drops over a small spill. From here, the main pull of water continues under the far bank for some thirty-five yards or more as it gradually slows to a more reasonable and steady pace. It then swings gently back to the centre of the river's coarse, and it is at this point, just as it begins to swing inwards, that a few bigger sea trout often lie, not near the surface but hard on the bottom. I would like to be able to wade a little closer to this bend in the current but the large rocks and the force of water make me think that it would not be such a good idea. The trick is to wade out to the edge of the spill and cast into the fast main current. Then, by paying line from the reel, I allow the current to carry the fly until it reaches the vital point. However, just in case any taking fish are lying in this fast run, the line is paid out as slowly as possible so that the fly appears to be attempting, at least, to swim against the current. I know exactly when this point is reached as I feel the start of the backing line. I now slowly retrieve the fly with a figure of eight motion, that is by coiling the line into my left hand. If there are no takers I repeat the same procedure over again. Sometimes a

sea trout will take here on the very first cast but, more usually, it is not until the fly has passed by some twenty times or more that one decides that enough is enough and has a go at it. Often, I have hooked a fish that felt heavy and set the adrenaline pumping until I felt it quickly weaken, telling me that it was a greedy chub.

I have tried many different patterns here, but the one that has rarely failed to catch me a sea trout has been the Medicine, and in particular one that was dressed with bead eyes.

I fished this Ribchester stretch one night in July 2002. I remember it well, not because I had a good night's fishing but because it was during the same evening that two so-called anglers made off with my favourite rod and landing net, which I had left leaning against the farmhouse garden wall. So much for the fraternity of anglers, but at least I know that the thieves were course and not game fishermen. Fortunately, I had spares and was able to continue.

As I walked up the bank I could see that the river was near perfect for sea trout fishing. Occasional fish were already starting to show all the way down towards Ribchester

55

Although the basic dressing is the same, this Medicine has bead eyes which help to balance the fly better and seem to attract more sea trout.

Bridge. By about 10pm it felt right to start, although without my usual lucky rod, and carrying a burden of anger, I was not feeling overly confident.

I tackled up with a sink tip line and a Medicine and waded through the shallower water until I was standing in the middle of the small spill that I mentioned above. I waited for a while, taking in my surroundings while studying the surface for any telltale signs of sea trout movement in the run below me. Suddenly, in the spot where the current swings, a big fish broke the surface. A sea trout or a salmon? I wasn't sure, but I had a certain feeling that this fish was a taker. I made a long cast into the fast water then paid off line, letting the pull of the current take the fly closer and ever closer to the magic spot. Telepathic messages were sent down the line. Please take.

The fly hung where I wanted it – the taking place. Go on, get hold of it. Any moment now and the current would swing it across the head of the bend and into the slacker water directly below me. I felt the line slacken, then bang! A fish had chased it as it swung out of the run. It was on and it was no chub. First it raced upstream towards me, too fast to keep in touch by reeling the line in. I had to hand strip, leaving a huge loop in the water by my feet. This is something to be avoided when playing a big fish, especially in the dark. I still suspected

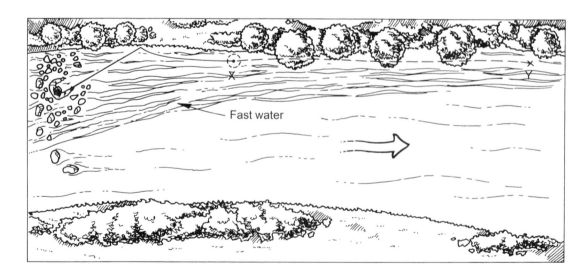

Figure 4. Letting out line. The fly is cast to position X and the line is very slowly paid out, letting the current carry the fly downstream to position Y. The fly is then retrieved as slowly as possible. This is also an ideal tactic when we wish the fly to pass under overhanging shrubs etc.

that this was indeed a salmon. When it was about ten yards from me it turned suddenly and shot back downstream at tremendous speed. But at least I no longer had to worry about the floating loop. Now it was tearing the backing line off but I couldn't follow it – it was far too dangerous here. The best I could do was pray. And then it leapt, a bar of angry silver shaking in the air. Please let the hook hold.

It crashed back down and took off again towards my bank and into an area filled with large underwater boulders. I applied side pressure in the hope of steering it towards the fast water. Better to fight it there than amongst the boulders. Fortunately it obliged and moved into the current some ten yards below my position. Then it stopped dead. I applied a steady pressure but nothing moved. I imagined that the cast must have become trapped amongst the rocks. I pulled harder – as hard as I dared – but it was solid. I kept the

pressure on and waited for what seemed ages. I was now convinced that the line was stuck and that the fish was probably long gone. I would have to tug until the leader snapped and start again. I pointed the rod towards the 'snag' and began to heave. Suddenly something moved. Had I hooked a sunken log? No; I felt the rod shake as the fish moved off. The fight was on again.

I managed to keep the fish in the fast water until I felt its strength begin to ebb and it was time to unclip the net. In it came, still fighting bravely to the last, until the net was slipped under it. This fish was one of the most beautiful specimens I have ever seen, a 6lb sea trout fresh up from the sea and covered in sea lice.

Sometime later I noticed that a fair number of sea trout were breaking the surface a little further downstream; not in a pool, but in what is best described as a continuation of the area I was currently fishing.

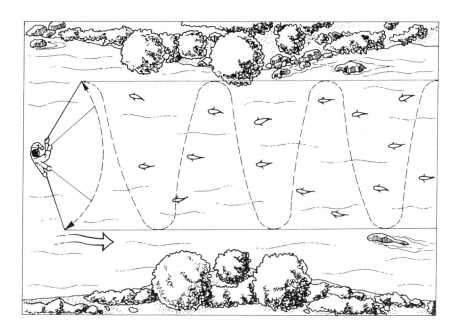

Figure 5. The area of water to be covered by fishing the zig-zag pattern.

But here there was a bit of a stipple on the surface caused by underwater rocks – what a sea angler might call rough ground. A good hiding place for wily sea trout. I also knew that getting into position over these fish would be fraught with difficulty, but nothing ventured, nothing gained. So I waded back to the shingle where I changed the sink tip for a floating line. No point in fishing too deep and risk getting caught up amongst the rocks.

I finally got into a reasonable position over the sea trout. Fortunately, they hadn't been disturbed by my wading and prodding, and now Mister Medicine and I were ready to do more business. With the sea trout still showing directly below me it was a good opportunity to fish the zig-zag method, a technique that can be used to cover a good area of water and which can be deadly. The stage by stage approach is described below.

When the rod is held out to the right (at arm's length if necessary) the line is collected by the current, causing the fly to swing from position X to position Y as the line straightens out (Figure 6). It is while the fly travels between X and Y that you are likely to get a take.

If you don't get a take, allow the fly to hang in position Y for twenty seconds or so and then take in about 3ft of line at a

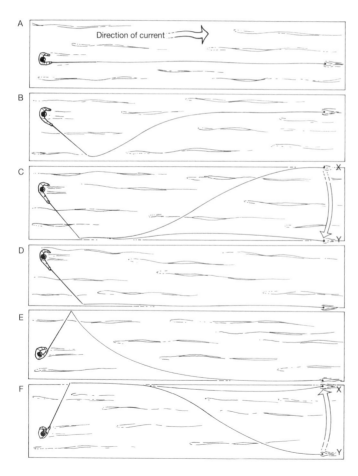

Figure 6. Zig-zag, the stage by stage technique. See text for instructions.

pace that is not too slow yet not too fast to appear unnatural. In other words, make the lure appear as though it was trying to make a short burst upstream. This will often induce a fish to chase and take. Let the fly hang in this position for a short period.

Now slowly swing the rod over to your left (changing hands if necessary to achieve a wider reach), let the current collect the line and swing the fly across to the left (from Y to X) until the line once again straightens out. Repeat the process until it is time to cast again.

To resume my story, I cast straight down the river and waited as the fly hung in the current. Nothing happened. I pushed the rod out to my right, waited until the fly swung across in line with the rod tip, then allowed it to hang in this position. Still no interest. I reeled in a yard of line and waited. Still nothing. I then slowly swung the rod across to my left and again waited for the current to collect the line and swing the fly to my left. This produced a take from a big chub that must have weighed well over 4lb. There are a lot of chub in this stretch but I never complain. I've been grateful for the fun I've had with these greedy rascals, especially on those nights when sea trout seemed few and far between.

Some ten minutes or so later, using the same zig-zag method, I got a good take from a fish that was lost almost as soon as it was hooked. But perseverance paid off and a little later a good sea trout was on and fighting like mad. Because of the hidden boulders, I knew that I had to keep the fish close to the surface. To achieve this it was necessary to keep the rod held as high as possible. But everything worked out well and a fit two pounder was soon in the net. This was later followed by another fish of a similar weight, then another a little smaller. This was good fun until I later got the urge to try my luck further down the river. I had often considered fishing this stretch but

had never got round to it. What the heck, if it didn't work out I still had a night to remember.

I waded back to the shingle, had a coffee and a cake, then made my way downstream in the direction of the bridge. I should have studied this next piece of water in greater detail. It was not as I had imagined it. Wading out to fish over what looked like a 'fishy' bit turned out to be precarious to say the least. It was filled with huge slippery boulders, slabs and deep potholes. By the time I eventually waded to my chosen spot it was well into the 'half-time' period and the fish had gone down for the night. Under normal circumstances, this would have been the time to change to a sinking line, but the river below me didn't seem too deep here. Besides, I didn't fancy wading all the way back to the bank so the floating line would have to do. However, I would still need to change the Medicine for something slightly heavier. I put my hand into my pocket to feel for my fly box. It wasn't there. I tried another pocket; not there either. I tried all my other pockets; no luck. I then fiddled about in my bag, but I still couldn't find it. I had no option but to switch on my head-light and take a good look inside the bag. It definitely wasn't there, but something shiny caught my eye. I fished out a Medi-cine; fortunately not the standard type but one I had tied on a double hook. Thinking it might just be heavy enough to get down to the fish, I tied it on.

With some dread I discovered that the flat rock I now stood on had a tendency to wobble. I could hear it clunk under my feet each time I shifted my balance. I did not feel safe but I was in no mood to give up now so I cast across the river and waited while the fly swung slowly round. A fish took – a big fish – and off it went with authority and the reel screaming. Then it happened. I lost my balance, the rock went clunk, and I went over in a kind of sideways dive with the water lapping round my chest and filling my waders. Needless to say, the fish was lost and I had learned a lesson the hard way. By luck, I later found my fly box on the bank, but now *I* needed some medicine – the twelve-year-old malt variety with hot water, a slice of lemon and a spoonful of sugar.

Here's the original Medicine pattern.

The dressing

Hooks	Size 4–1/0 low-water Wilson
Silk	Red
Body	Flat silver to cover three-quarters of the upper shank
Rib	Fine oval silver or silver wire (optional)
Hackle	Blue tied in false. The shade known as 'teal' blue is best
Wing	A flank feather from a teal or widgeon. Select one with distinctive black and white stripes. The wing should be slim and lie close to the body
Head	Red

JOE PYE

This fly was developed many years ago when I used to fish the River Hodder on a regular basis. Originally it was dressed with a short body on a size 8 long shank hook to combat those sea trout that are inclined to tweak at the rear end of the fly rather than take with determination; a frustratingly frequent occurrence on the River Hodder in the late summer months when the river is low and clear.

Dressing a fly with a short body is a common ploy in sea trout fishing; the idea being to induce the fish to nip the fly higher up the hook, at the base of the body, and consequently find itself hooked. For the reasons given below, this fly was later dressed in the more traditional fashion, with a full-length body on a Kamasan low-water salmon hook. This too has proved its worth on the River Hodder and has also been a winner on many other rivers, although it is not as good at hooking tweaking fish as the original version.

A big sea trout leaping the weir on the River Tyne at Hexham.

Sadly, it has become increasingly difficult to obtain fishing on the middle and lower part of this river in recent years, at least fishing that I can afford.

If there was ever the perfect game fishing river then it has to be the Hodder. It is a river most fly fishermen see in their dreams. From its source high in the Trough of Bowland, it tumbles down the fell to the picturesque village of Slaidburn, where time has stood still for the past five hundred years, where the scenery is rugged and dramatic and the folks are friendly and laid back. Good food and beers can be had in the Hark and Bounty and the best bacon barm and pot of tea is available from the little riverside café by the old stone bridge. For a modest sum you can purchase a permit from the local post office to fish for salmon, trout, grayling and sea trout, and although it is often very late in the season before the sea trout and salmon arrive, the summer grayling fishing can often be excellent.

From Slaidburn, the river winds its way towards the ancient village of Newton, passing through the easy to fish sheep-cropped meadows of Dunnow Hall, then on through more spectacular countryside to Dunsop Bridge where it is joined by the tiny River Dunsop and Langden Brook. This is walkers country, where shy roe deer wander and buzzards soar.

From here the river runs on towards the enchanting tiny village of Whitewell, which consists of a few stone cottages, the hotel and the tiny parish church of St Michael.

The river then runs through dense forest and moor towards the secretive village of Bashall Eaves, where you could once get a day permit from the Red Pump, but not any longer. From here the river makes its way towards Mitton, where it enters the River Ribble at Hodder Foot. Every mile of the Hodder offers something new and

A great sea trout holding pool on the River Hodder. In the late evening sea trout will often congregate at the head of the lower pool and once it is dark enough they will run up into the higher pool.

61

special for the eye to behold. This is certainly one of the most unspoiled valleys in Britain and my only hope is that it will remain so. But it is to Whitewell where my memories take me.

In the 'golden age' I would frequently stay at the Whitewell Hotel, which has now changed its name to The Inn at Whitewell. In those days, accommodation was very reasonable and there was always a rod available for guests. Today, however, I would have to dig deep into my piggy bank before I could revisit my old haunt. The Hodder here forms the border between the two counties of Yorkshire and Lancashire and until recently, in historic terms, it seems that the Battle of the Roses continued to be fought.

One fine summer day found me fishing the pool just a little way upstream of the hotel, where I was enjoying some good sport with brown trout to a dry fly. I watched two teenage boys, who were quite obviously farmer's lads, cross the field on the opposite bank and with crude tackle and a jam jar full of worms they began to fish. From their side of the river, however, they were having difficulty in preventing their offerings from being swept under the bank. I could see their frustration, so I called to them and suggested that if they went a little way upstream to where the river was shallow they could paddle across and fish my side with much less effort. The oldest lad looked at me as if I had taken leave of my senses. 'We daren't go o'er theer' he called back. Surely no one would object to two lads drowning a few worms. 'Why not?' I asked.

'Me dad'ud kill us.'

'How's that?' I enquired, somewhat mystified.

Dead serious, he shouted back, 'That's Yorkshire o'er yon side mister.'

Ideal sea trout water. During the day sea trout will lie in the fast water. At night some fish will drop back in the pool while others will run. Both can be caught in the tail of the pool just above the white water.

At that time the gamekeeper's name was Joe Pye, a rum old character who lived in a cottage close to the hotel. Joe was, and forever will be, a legend on the River Hodder. Joe loved his job and his whisky, although in which order I am unsure. He was a giant of a man in every sense of the word, squarely built with a deep gruff voice that would easily scare any poacher half to death. He was one of those genuine old-timers that one only occasionally comes across and never forgets. He had been a gamekeeper in these parts for as long as anyone could remember. In fact, he had been a keeper from the age of eight when he took over the job from his father. What Joe didn't know about the countryside wasn't worth knowing. Unfortunately, he is no longer with us but he will never be forgotten along the Hodder Valley. There are many stories told about him, but this one is worth relating.

Some years ago my Aunt Helen, who I had a great affection for, died suddenly while still in her early forties. There had been no indication that she was ill. In fact, she had seemed in good health except for a stomach complaint, which no one, including herself, had realised the seriousness of. Naturally, her passing away was a great shock to my immediate family and, of course, to my Uncle Bob, her husband.

After a few months had passed by, I thought it would be a good idea to take Uncle Bob fishing and decided that the Whitewell Hotel would be a nice place to go. Naturally, I was pleased when he agreed to join me. Although he was more into coarse fishing than game fishing, he thought it would do him good to get away from the house for a while.

We spent a very enjoyable few days fishing. He caught some nice sea trout on a spinner while I did well on the fly. On our last day we rose a little before dawn and made our way down the river to fish some pools that we had not yet tried. But the going was tough and we had to fight our way through a jungle of tall grasses, fern and giant hogweed. It was something of a safari, but the fishing was worth it. I took a 3lb sea trout within the first few minutes, just as the first hint of light was beginning to peep over the fell. But all good things have to come to an end and by 9am it was time to pack up, pay our bill, and set off on the long journey home.

Later in the day we arrived outside my uncle's house. As we sat in the car he thanked me, saying that the experience had done him good. But I got the impression that he was uneasy about entering the house alone, so I suggested I went in with him and make us a cuppa. Yes, he liked the idea of that, but as we neared his door and he put his hand in his pocket to take out his keys, I saw the colour drain from him. His keys were missing. But more than that, the keys had been attached to a heart-shaped gold locket of much sentimental value that contained a photograph of Aunt Helen. I could imagine his pain.

Fortunately, he had a spare key and as we sat drinking tea I asked him if he could remember the last time he had seen the keys. He remembered it had been in the middle of the 'jungle'. He had stopped to look at the photograph inside the locket.

I thought it would do no harm to phone the hotel – just in case. But I knew that the chances of them being handed in were slim. No, the keys had not been handed in, the manager told me. I waited while someone went to search our bedrooms. No keys there either. In fact, it was very unlikely that the keys had been mislaid in the hotel or someone would have found them by now. 'Where did he have them last' he asked. I told him. 'Bloody hell,' he replied, 'It's like Brazil down there.' I thanked him for his trouble and left Uncle Bob's phone number just in case. 'Tell you what,' he said, 'I'll have a word with old Joe – tell him to keep his eye open for them.'

I thanked him and put down the phone.

Around noon the following day, Uncle Bob received a call from the hotel to say that Joe had found the keys complete with locket. Without delay we set off for White-well, where we found the old man sat at the bar with a twinkle in his eye and a whisky in his hand. Sure enough, the keys had been dropped in the 'jungle' and I was interested to know how, amongst such dense vegetation, he had managed to find them.

'Easy,' he replied, 'I just kept my eye on the magpies. They're attracted to bright things, don't y'know.'

That cost us more than a few drams, but it was worth it.

A few weeks later I was walking down the river on a hot evening. As I made my way through a clump of bushes, my nose caught a bad smell. Then I came across Joe, who was sat leaning against a dead tree. With his familiar battered trilby half hanging off his head, his tattered wellies lying in the grass and his big toes poking through holes in each of his socks – the obvious source of the smell – it was one of those occasions when I wished I had had a camera. As we chatted, Joe began to scrape the muck from his fingernails with a piece of stick. 'Well, you can't go for a drink wi' shitty nails, can you?' He had a point, although I was aware that he was trying to drop a hint, a hint that I intentionally allowed to fall on deaf ears. I was going fishing and wasn't going to let Joe delay me any longer. 'What's that fly you've got on then?'

I showed him and asked him what he thought of it.

The tail of the pool on a stream in mid-Wales. The author has taken many good sea trout in this spot.

'Bloody rubbish' he growled. 'It needs some red in its arse.'

I couldn't help laughing, but the following day – just to please Joe – I tied up the same fly with a red tag. It worked. In fact, it worked so well that I had a 4lb sea trout on it that night along with six more of around 2lb.

When I next saw Joe I told him that I had changed the fly slightly on his advice and about how well I had done on it. Typical of Joe, he wasted no time in reminding me that the bar would soon be open. 'Worth a drink is that. I tawd thee, see I tawd thee – red in its arse.' I was wishing I'd kept my big mouth shut. An hour or so later, after Joe had told me a number of country tales (most of which I had heard before) and after his tonsils had been well lubricated and I was wishing I was on the river, Joe suggested that I should name the fly after him. He suggested Joe Pye's Red Arse. I think plain Joe Pye will do just as well.

The dressing

Hooks	6–1/0 Kamasan B180 low-water salmon
Silk	Red
Body	First a short tag of bright red seal's fur, or substitute, followed by white antron chenille (or white sparkle chenille)
Rib	Medium round gold of copper wire over the chenille only
Hackle	Red cock hackle fibres tied in false at the throat
Wing	Mixed white and brown natural bassarisk tail fibres (or squirrel)
Head	Black with white eyes

While researching this book I was kindly given much information by local fishermen along the Hodder Valley. So much information, in fact, that I could probably write an entire book about this wonderful river. Regrettably, I am confined to space and can

A quiet and deeper pool on the River Lune. Here sea trout lie close to the bank under the cover of overhanging bushes. It was under this very bush that the author took a 5lb sea trout on a Joe Pye.

65

only use a small part of it. Almost without exception, everyone I spoke to mentioned a particular old pattern that has a reputation as a killer of salmon and sea trout on the Hodder, yet it seems to be unheard of elsewhere. This is the Stonyhurst Black, and for those who would like to try it, the pattern is given below.

The dressing

Hook	Size 4–1/0 Wilson low-water salmon
Silk	Black
Tail	Golden pheasant tippet
Body	Black silk floss
Rib	Round, or oval silver tinsel
Hackle	A double hackle of blue and crimson cock
Wing	Brown turkey
Head	Black

A fresh 2¹/₂lb sea trout from the River Kent. This one fell to a Tammy Troot in August when the river was very low.

TAMMY TROOT

This fly was originally designed as a trout rather than a sea trout lure. Its purpose is to represent a small brown trout. I have taken many brown and rainbow trout on it, but it was not until recent years that I tried tying it in larger sizes as a sea trout fly. I was surprised to find that it worked extremely well, particularly in the early hours of darkness when the river is low. You may wish to try tying this one for yourself. The dressing is a little unconventional, which is why I have given instructions in addition to the dressing.

The dressing

Hooks	Size 6 or 8 Kamasan B180 low-water salmon hook
Silk	Black
Body	Silver tinsel with peacock herl over, to form the tail
Rib	Fine oval silver
Hackle	Black cock hackle fibres tied in as false beard
Wing	First red cock hackle fibres with black cock hackle fibres over
Head	Black

After you have tied on a bed of tying silk, catch in the rib above the bend. Now catch in the flat tinsel and wind this up to the eye to form the first part of the body.

Behind the eye, tie in a few strands of peacock herl to point forward. Now bring the herl back over the body and tie it down by winding the rib over and up towards the eye to hold the herl in place. Now snip off the herl to leave a short stumpy tail.

You can now tie in the throat hackle followed by the wing and finish off at the head, which is varnished black. Alternatively, you may wish to give the fly added appeal by painting on a pair of white eyes.

FOXON'S FAVOURITES

Arthur Foxon owns a fishing tackle shop in St Asaph in North Wales. This is not just any old tackle shop, but a game fishing tackle shop that is so well stocked it would take you all morning to have a good look round. It is an Aladdin's cave. As for Arthur, you couldn't wish to meet a more likeable or helpful chap. He is an authority on game fishing, especially sea trout fishing. He has the Castle Beat on the River Clwyd, which is a sea trout angler's dream.

I could say much more about Arthur and about his generosity and the help he has given me in writing this book. But I cannot mention Arthur without also mentioning his charming wife Rosalind, who is recognised as one of the best fly dressers in Wales. Rosalind kindly sent me three of her own creations, which have proved deadly, not only on the Clwyd but on other rivers throughout the UK. These are Silent Night, Dusk and REF, the latter being Rosalind's initials: Rosalind Elinor Foxon. The dressings are given below. Each of these flies works exceedingly well when the last embers of the day have all but merged into night. They also make excellent use of the Partridge Salar hooks that, as well as the standard black, are also manufactured in a silver and gold finish.

Silent Night dressing

Hooks	Size 6 or 8 Partridge Salar (silver)
Silk	Black
Body	First a short tag of green holo graphic flat tinsel, then flat red tinsel
Rib	Fine oval silver
Hackle	Black cock hackle fibres tied in at the throat
Wing	Black squirrel tail fibres with a few strands of red and pearl mirror flash over
Head	Black

Dusk on the River Ribble. This picture was taken in July when the river was on its bones yet full of sea trout.

Dusk dressing

Hooks	Size 6 or 8 Partridge Salar (silver)
Silk	Black
Body	First a short tag of flat blue holographic tinsel followed by a short tag of red holographic tinsel. This is continued with the same blue holographic tinsel
Rib	Fine oval silver
Hackle	Medium blue cock hackle fibres tied in at the throat
Wing	Mixed strands of yellow, black and brown squirrel tail fibres. Then a few strands of crystal mirror flash over
Head	Black

REF dressing

Hooks	Size 6 or 8 Partridge Salar (gold)
Silk	Black
Body	A short tag of green holographic tinsel followed by gold holographic tinsel
Rib	Fine oval silver
Wing	Black squirrel tail fibres with just two strands of green crystal mirror flash over
Hackle	Orange cock hackle wound on after the wing has been tied in. Unlike the first two, this is not tied in false; it is wound on last to form a throat hackle and the upper part the wing
Head	Black

JESSICA

This is a fly that I have used more recently with much success. Again, it is a great little fly to use in the early hours of darkness. It is a simple fly to dress because it has no wing, just a hackle and a body that even a child could tie. In fact, the one shown in the colour section was tied for me by my granddaughter Jessica when she was just ten years old. I doubt she would forgive me if I didn't mention her here, and she will be thrilled to see her name in this book.

I have six lovely grandchildren, all of whom I am greatly proud of. I would have expected one of my grandsons to be mad about fishing as both I and my son Chris are. However, it was Jessica who emerged as the fishing fanatic; she just loves fishing of any kind and, in particular, fly fishing.

When Jessica was only seven, Chris and I took her sea fishing to North Wales. We two men, the so-called experts, caught nothing but Jessica caught two beautiful fat flounders.

A few weeks later Chris and I took her sea fishing once again and it was almost a repeat of the first time. The men blanked while Jessica caught a conger eel.

On holiday in Cornwall, when Jessica was eight, Chris decided to get up very early to sneak in a couple of hours at Porthoustock. But Jessica was wide-awake and there was no way she was going to be left behind. Chris didn't even get a bite but Jessica caught a beautiful bass, which we all had for tea.

Later in the year I took her fly fishing on Stocks Reservoir in Lancashire. There was no way that Jessica was going to beat me at my own specialised game – but she did. Within an hour she had got the hang of casting like a duck to water. My best fish for the day weighed 2lb but Jessica's was 3½lb.

For Christmas she requested a fly fishing outfit, which I bought. For her birthday, a fly tying kit of course.

I was invited by Karl Humphries to fish Dearnford Hall lake in Shropshire where he is the manager. Jessica, now aged ten, and on her way to becoming something of an expert, wanted to come along too.

We had a wonderful day fishing from a boat and caught a few nice fish (Jessica, of course, caught the biggest), but for the last hour we decided to fish from the bank. As I was tying the boat up to the little jetty I got into conversation with two elderly gentlemen who told me that they had been there all day without so much as a pluck. Jessica, who was stood close by, did no more than cast in and caught a 2lb rainbow right away. The two anglers looked on in amazement as she played her fish. One remarked that he had never seen a kid so full of enthusiasm – especially a girl – and couldn't she cast well too. I swelled with pride. 'Yes, she's my granddaughter.'

The dressing

Hooks	6, 8 or 10 Partridge Salar or low-water Wilson
Silk	Black
Body	Black seal's fur teased out slightly
Rib	Red enameled copper wire. A few tight turns to start forming a short tag, then continued round the body
Hackle	Black cock hackle
Head	Black with white eyes and red pupils

Incidentally, I acquired the red copper wire from a company that manufactures electrical coils.

The author fishing the Castle Beat on the River Clwyd. Here the level is affected by the flooding and ebbing of the tide.

7   Doubles and Trebles

While flies dressed on double or treble hooks certainly have greater hooking potential, it has been claimed that their use is unsporting because they are more difficult to remove and consequently cause more harm. While avoiding a wider debate on this issue, I can only say that personally I have never had too much trouble in removing a fly dressed on a double or treble hook from a fish, especially as I always use forceps and treat the fish with respect. In fact, I am unable to think of a single occasion when I returned a fish caught on such a fly that did not recover and swim away none the worse for the experience. I would, however, con-

tend that to use such a hook in bait fishing is strictly taboo and that the chances of removing even a single hook from a fish that has taken the bait deep down, without causing some injury, is a slim one. But as a fly fisherman, I think I would defend the right to dress flies on such hooks.

There are also those who say that they get less offers when using flies dressed on such hooks and here they may have a point. A fly that did not have any hook at all, in other words a fly dressed simply on a shank, would, I'm sure, get plenty of offers. Unfortunately, if we wish to catch a fish then the fly must have a hook. We know that a real fish or sedge, or whatever we seek to imitate, does not have a hook under or behind it. We fish in the hope that the fish we intend to catch will not notice the hook, only the dressing. So one single hook is less noticeable than two and much less noticeable than three, therefore the single-hook dressing will get more attention. But what if we dressed a fly that made no attempt to disguise the hook? This is more easy with a treble hook. The points become the tail of a small fish or legs or feelers, which point forward, thus arousing a fish's curiosity. The same could be said for dressing our treble or double using a silver or gold hook, or one painted white. The hook becomes part of the 'flash' that attracts and triggers the sea trout's feeding, curiosity or aggressive instincts rather than its acute suspicion.

Two such patterns that you might like to try for yourself are given next.

Double (top) and treble (bottom) hook dressings of the Medicine.

THE GREEN IMP

This is a small fly that I have used very successfully in the first few hours of darkness and during the day when the water was in spate or stained. It might be worth making the point here that the usual theory of using a bigger fly in spate conditions is not always the case. A small bright fly such as this one will often work much better than some larger flies. I recall once going to fish the River Irt in Cumbria when it was coming down like drinking chocolate. Other local anglers were either spinning or worming but I hadn't expected to find the river up and had only brought fly tackle. Naturally, it had to be a fast sinking line to get the fly down, but which fly? When I looked into my fly box some sixth sense made me choose the small Green Imp and, although it seemed something of a ridiculous choice, I stayed with my initial instinct and put it on. The result was ten sea trout between 1 and 4lb.

The dressing

Hook	Size 14 Partridge X2B long shank treble hook
Silk	Red
Body	Fluorescent lime green chenille
Hackle	Pale natural ginger cock hackle
Rib	Fine copper wire
Wing	None
Head	Red

KARL'S BLUE AND SQUIRREL

This dressing is a variation of the tried and tested Blue and Squirrel, of which there are countless interpretations. But the one here, which is dressed by Karl Humphries, is one that I have a particular liking for. Although at the time of writing I have yet to try it myself, I am assured that on the majority of Welsh rivers it has gained something of a reputation.

The dressing

Hooks	Size 6 or 8 lightweight double
Silk	Black
Tail	A short stump of pale fluorescent blue floss
Body	Holographic silver tinsel
Rib	Fine round silver
Hackle	Guinea fowl dyed medium-blue tied in false at the throat
Cheeks	Jungle cock
Wing	Natural grey squirrel tail
Head	Black

BLUE AND SILVER

It would be impossible not to include the Blue and Silver; it is probably the most popular sea trout and salmon dressing of all time. It is also recognised as a Medicine, except it is dressed here on a treble or double hook depending on your choice.

The dressing

Hooks	Size 16–6 Partridge 02 double Wilson, or size 16–8 Partridge X2B long shank treble
Silk	Red
Body	Flat silver, plain or holographic
Rib	Silver wire
Hackle	Light or 'teal' blue as in the Medicine. The hackle is tied under rather than round it, as in most flies dressed on double or treble hooks
Wing	Teal, same as the Medicine
Head	Red

THE ROYAL MEDICINE

This dressing, which was given to me by Karl Humphries, is again a version of the Blue and Silver. It is the luxury version, and a very striking fly. Unsurprisingly, Karl has caught many sea trout on it. Look in the colour section to see what a stunning fly it is.

The dressing

Hooks	Size 16–6 Partridge 02 double Wilson, or size 16–8 Partridge XB2 long shank treble
Silk	Red
Body	Flat silver, plain or holographic
Wing	Fibres of turkey marabou dyed royal blue tied in sparingly. Over this are a few well-marked teal fibres. The wing is dressed all round the hook, unlike the above fly
Cheeks	Jungle cock
Head	Red

RED MAXWELL

This pattern was first dressed by a self-confessed lazy fly dresser by the name of Rod Maxwell, who I used to fish with on the River Annan. It is a fly that makes no attempt whatsoever to hide the hook. Rod's theory, and I think he may have a point (if you'll pardon the pun), is that sea trout like the shape of a treble hook and are attracted by it. So basic is this fly that it doesn't even have a wing, but Rod never seemed to have any trouble catching fish on it and neither did I. We spent many long nights on the river and caught many fish on his sparsely dressed flies.

The dressing

Hooks	Size 8–10 long shank treble
Silk	Black
Body	Flat red tinsel
Rib	Fine or medium oval silver
Hackle	A cock hackle dyed crimson-red tied in palmer style over the body only
Wing	None
Head	Black

For the hackle, the fibres are stripped from one side of the feather and tied in at the finest point before the red body tinsel and the oval ribbing tinsel are caught in. After winding on the red tinsel, the hackle is then wound on up to the eye. The rib is then wound on in the opposite direction to the hackle, thus crossing over the hackle and securing it in place at the same time.

In August 2004 Rod wrote to me to say that over the past couple of seasons he had started dressing some sea trout flies with just a hackle on a bare gold or silver-finished long shank treble hook and that he had enjoyed considerable success on them. I'm not convinced that this is the start of something big, but it does leave some food for thought.

8 Tube Flies

The advent of the tube fly was something of a revolution as far as salmon fishing was concerned, particularly on bigger rivers such as the Tay, Tweed and Spey. Naturally, it was soon realised that tube flies also took sea trout, especially when fished in heavier and faster water that will work the fly and give it a resemblance of life. There are arguable advantages and disadvantages.

Advantages
The treble hook provides greater hooking potential.
The tube will usually shoot clear of the hook, thus providing the fish with less chance of levering itself free.
If a hook is snapped or becomes blunted it is a simple matter just to change the treble.
They are easy to dress as they usually consist of nothing more than hair tied around the tube.

Disadvantages
Heavier brass tubes are more difficult to cast.
The hook sometimes becomes free of the sleeve and sticks out awkwardly at an angle.
The hook is inclined to catch over the leader, especially in windy conditions.
The weight of the treble makes it swim bottom down in slacker water.

The body tube materials are usually aluminium or brass, which have a plastic liner, and plastic, thus providing a variety of weights to suit a variety of conditions.

This also means that the sink rate is easily regulated by selecting either of these three materials. A small dressing on a ½in plastic tube, for instance, would be suitable for fishing the streamier runs of a smaller river at summer level, possibly changing up to a ¾in aluminium tube if there was a small rise of the same water. Brass tubes are used less often in sea trout fishing, their main use being for spring and back end salmon fishing when the river is often higher. However, there have been occasions when I did make use of a short brass tube for sea trout

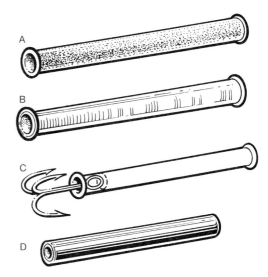

Figure 7. Types of tubes for tube flies. (A) A plastic tube with moulded ends to prevent the dressing slipping off. (B) Aluminium tube with a plastic lining. (C) A larger plastic tube with a cavity at the rear to house the treble hook. (D) A brass tube with a plastic lining for heavier flies.

when I needed to get the fly down while fishing in fast and fierce water.

Unlike hooks, tubes cannot be fixed in the vice, so here are a few tips that the novice might find helpful.

Lined tubes

Fix your dubbing needle in the vice and simply push on the tube until the lining grips the needle tightly. Alternatively, cut the eye off a hook and sharpen the shank with a file. Fix the hook in the vice and push the tube on until it fits tight (*see* Figure 8A).

Unlined tubes

Push the end of a long needle of the appropriate size through the tube, then through a piece of rubber (such as a pencil eraser), which will protect the end of the tube from any damage that might be caused by the jaws of the vice.

Now pull the point of the needle into the jaws of the vice with a pair of pliers and tighten the vice to hold everything in place (*see* Figure 8B).

Plastic tubes

For plastic tubes, I have used tubing from a variety of sources. You can buy purpose-made tubes with moulded ends, which will be helpful in the process of dressing and will prevent the dressing from slipping off. In addition, you can now purchase tubes with a recessed section at one end into which the eye of the treble hook fits. Alternatively, I have used all manner of discarded items, from a lollipop stick to ballpoint pen refills.

If the tube is not recessed to accommodate the eye of the treble, then you will need to make use of a sleeve to keep the treble aligned with the body. This is usually a short piece of silicone or rubber tubing, which is pushed on to the end of the tube and into which fit's the eye of the treble. But a note of caution. I have known some anglers who have dressed their tube flies using shrink wrap tubing to house the treble. This might be okay if no heat is applied to it, but when it is, and the tubing is shrunk about the eye of the treble, this will prevent the body shooting clear of the hook and will offer the fish a greater chance of levering itself free. Some anglers never bother to use anything to house the treble,

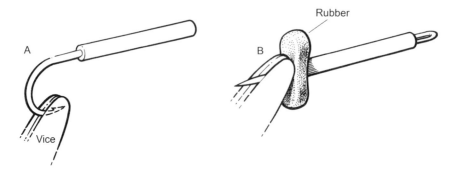

Figure 8. (A) A hook, with the eye snipped off and sharpened, is pushed into the end of the plastic-lined tube to hold it securely in the vice. (B) With unlined tubes, a darning needle is pushed through the tube, then through a piece of rubber before it is locked tightly in the vice.

but how they expect the fly to swim right, let alone catch fish, is beyond me.

When dressing the tube fly, it will be helpful if provision is made to accommodate the sleeve. This is done by dressing the body so that a short piece at the end of the tube remains bare. This way, the sleeve can easily be pushed onto the tube (*see* Figure 9). By dressing the complete body of the tube you might encounter difficulty in fitting the sleeve and cause damage to the dressing. In addition, a sleeve that is pushed on over the dressing will make the fly bulky at its rear end and therefore unattractive and clumsy-looking.

In giving you some useful dressings, you will note that I have not attempted to say which type of tube you should use, as there may be a number of conditions under which the same dressing is fished. The best I can do is give you the following general indication of what my likely tactics would be on most of the typical sea trout rivers that I fish.

The table below is only a general indication that might be of some help. On bigger and heavier waters, larger and heavier tubes

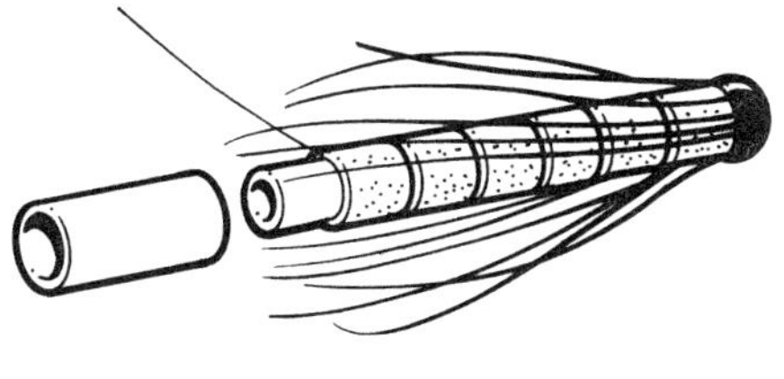

End dressing here to allow for sleeve

Figure 9. Dressing the tube fly. See text for instructions.

of up to 1½in or more might be better. But every water is different on different days and there is no definite rule regarding the weight and size of the tube fly. One must learn to read the water on the day and make one's own judgement.

On the subject of size, there is one simple way to lengthen the fly and add weight, which is known as a 'double tube'. Quite simply, all you need to do is slide one tube on to the line above another. This can often be a deadly way to catch fish, both sea trout and salmon. Moreover, it allows the angler a wide scope in his choice of

Dead low summer level. Slow to medium speed	Plastic	¼in, size 16 treble
	Plastic	½in, size 16 treble
	Plastic	¾in, size 14 treble
A slight rise in the water. Medium speed	Plastic	¾in, size 14 treble
	Plastic	1in, size 12 treble
	Aluminium	¾in, size 14 treble
	Aluminium	1in, size 12 treble
	Aluminium	1¼in, size 12 treble
Water running off after a spate. Medium to fast speed	Aluminium	1¼in, size 12 treble
	Brass	1in, size 12 treble
	Brass	1¼in, size 12 treble

pattern combinations. For example, I have caught a number of good fish on a Teal and Silver dressing that had a Stoat Tail dressing below it (*see* Figure 10).

Eyes

I have mentioned throughout this book how lures that feature eyes can make a difference to fish catches and I see no reason why tube flies should not feature them. A simple tip is to paint on three eyes at equal distance around the head of the fly. This way at least one eye is seen no matter what angle the fish sees the fly from.

Hooks

Do not use needle-eye treble hooks as they will be too slack inside the sleeve. The best I can recommend are the Partridge Standard Treble Hooks. One last tip, to lighten the fly you could easily change the hook for a double, or even a single if you so wish.

Riffling

Not long ago, when out after salmon on the River Leven, I was joined by my good friend Chris Slater, the bailiff, who invited me round to his house for a brew after I had finished. But first I had to catch a salmon. After much hard work, I eventually did – a nice fish of about 8lb that, I hasten to add, was returned safely to the river to spawn in the hope of better seasons to come.

Having got that out of my system, I called round at my friend's house where his good wife, Carol, was already in the process of preparing the sloes for the sloe gin that, hopefully, would be ready in time for the Christmas festivities. Carol's sloe gin has to be tried to be believed – it is superb! It goes without saying that the talk got round to fishing and in the course of the conversation the subject of tube flies came up. Chris then showed me some of his own dressings. I was particularly intrigued with a simple idea that will add much life to the fly. Here it is.

Dress the fly on a plastic tube leaving a short piece above the head bare. Now heat the point of your dubbing needle and push it through the side of the tube to make a hole just above the head of the fly. When fishing it, instead of feeding the leader straight through the tube in the normal way, the leader is first pushed

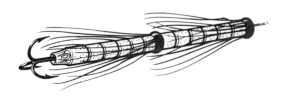

Figure 10. The 'double tube'. An easy way to lengthen the lure by adding one tube fly above the other.

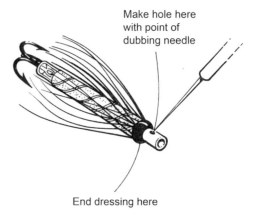

Make hole here with point of dubbing needle

End dressing here

Figure 11. Dressing a fly for 'riffling'. See text for instructions.

A good run on the Cumbrian Leven, perfect for 'riffling'.

A tube fly ready for 'riffling'.

through the hole you have made and then continued through the tube before tying on the hook (*see* Figure 11). This will now cause the fly, which should be fished on a floating line, to skitter in a frenzied action about the surface in a method known as 'riffling'. This is achieved by allowing the fly to hang in the current, or by retrieving it. The action of the fly is difficult to describe – it has to be seen to be believed – it is deadly!

Tube fly dressings are endless and I could probably fill an entire book with them. The few I have given below are the ones which I have been inclined to use in more recent years.

SILVER DOG

Silk	Black
Body	Flat holographic silver
Rib	Silver wire
Wing	Black squirrel tail. A few red dyed cock hackle fibres are tied in over this
Head	Black
Eyes	White with red centres. Three eyes are painted on at equal distance around the head. (*See* under 'eyes' above)

BLACK GORDON

This deadly pattern, which uses black deer hair in the wing, is more suited to shorter patterns.

Silk	Black
Body	Black silk floss
Rib	Silver wire, or size 14 oval silver in longer sizes

Wing	Black deer hair (the kind normally used to make some Muddler patterns) with a few strands of green Krystal Flash mixed in
Head	Black
Eyes	Optional. *See* above pattern for Silver Dog

ALEXANDRA

This is an adaptation of the famous fly.

Silk	Black
Body	Flat holographic silver
Rib	Silver wire
Wing	Strands of olive Krystal Flash with a few red dyed cock hackle fibres over
Head	Black
Eyes	Optional

HIGH VIZ

This pattern, which is designed for use in higher water that might be stained, particularly by peat, is best dressed on longer tubes of 1½ to 2in.

Silk	Yellow
Body	Flat holographic silver
Rib	Silver wire, or size 14 oval silver in longer patterns
Wing	White buck with strands of gold Krystal Flash mixed in
Head	Yellow
Eyes	Black with white centres

The beauty of dressing tube flies is that it allows scope for tying up a vast range of different patterns. Have fun.

9 Some Old Favourites

The flies described so far have, for the most part, been 'modern' flies. Some have been my own inventions while others are, or have been based on, the creations of others who have given the subject considerable thought over the course of many years of successful sea trout fishing. Although most of the flies I use today are second generation, there are still a few old favourites that I would not like to be without. These are all excellent river flies, particularly in the early part of the night.

Obviously, we all have our own favourite 'traditionals' and it would be foolish of me to suggest that the flies given below are better than any other – they are simply the

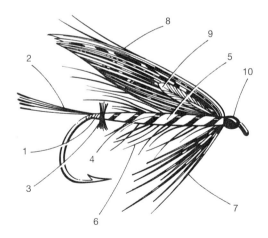

Figure 12. Parts of a fly. A fully dressed traditional wet fly pattern, although very few dressings would feature all the parts named. 1. Tag. 2. Tail. 3. Butt. 4. Body. 5. Rib. 6. Body hackle. 7. Throat hackle. 8. Wing. 9. Sides. 10. Head.

ones in which I personally have the most confidence.

THE HASLAM

No list of sea trout flies could ever be complete without the Haslam. This unique fly, which features horns, is very much regarded as a 'traditional' and is, without doubt, one of the greatest sea trout flies of all time, and one which seems to take sea trout both by day and night. I was never quite sure what it was supposed to represent, although having a silver body, I have a feeling that sea trout are inclined to see it as a small fish, particularly when the horns are caused to twitch in such a tantalising way, thus adding extra 'life'. Or do they see it as something else? Perhaps this is a fly that arouses the sea trout's curiosity as much as my own.

The fly illustrated on page 80 was tied by none other than that world-famous fly dresser, Sid Knight of Bridgenorth. Keeping up with modern materials, Sid has used holographic rather than the traditional silver tinsel for the body, which is an improvement as far as I am concerned. Not only does it reflect more light, it also serves to make the fly more attractive, not just to me, but the sea trout too. Sid has also used a pale grey body hackle, which I think adds further attraction to this fly and, in addition, he has replaced the butt of white wool with phosphorescent strip wound on in place. When held under the light of a torch

Two hopeful visitors from Germany fishing on the River Dovey, the home of the Haslam.

The Haslam as dressed by Sid Knight.

for a while the phosphorescent butt will glow in the dark adding further attraction.

The first Haslam I ever received was dressed by Peter Vaughan of Machynlleth. He was a close and long-standing friend of Dr Haslam who invented this amazing fly. It is a particular favourite on most Welsh rivers and, in particular, the River Dovey (Dyfi) where I have spent many enjoyable days, and nights too, and where I have caught a good many beautiful sewin on this very fly.

There are a number of variations of the Haslam but, as far as I know, this is the original as created by Dr Haslam. To any Welshmen who might think otherwise, I apologise now.

The (original) dressing

Hooks	4, 6, 8 or 10 Partridge single low water. This is also a good fly dressed on a double Salar hook up to size 1 or even 10 when a heavier fly is required or when salmon is your quarry
Silk	Black
Tag	A short tag of flat silver tinsel as in the body
Butt	White wool or white ostrich herl
Tail	A golden pheasant crest feather
Body	Flat silver tinsel
Rib	None
Hackle	Blue jay, or dyed guinea fowl for larger flies
Horns	Two blue macaw fibres (or substitute)
Wing	Hen pheasant tail
Head	Black

Sid Knight's dressing

Hooks	4, 6, 8 or 10 Partridge single low water (as above)
Silk	Black
Tag	Flat holographic silver tinsel
Butt	A thin strip of phosphorescent tape is wound on to form the butt
Tail	A golden pheasant crest feather
Body	Flat holographic silver

80

Rib	Silver wire size 14 oval silver on larger flies
Hackle	(Body) A hen hackle dyed pale grey
Hackle	(Throat) Blue jay fibres (dyed guinea fowl in larger flies)
Horns	Blue macaw tail fibres (or substitute)
Head	Black

Construction (Sid Knight's dressing)

1 Wind on a bed of tying silk from the eye to the bend and catch in a length of fine round silver.

2 Now catch in a short length of medium flat holographic silver tinsel and make about two turns towards the eye to form a short tag. Tie this in and snip off the excess.

3 Now catch in a thin strip of phosphorescent tape and wind this in to form the short butt. Tie this down and snip off the excess.

4 A single golden pheasant crest feather is now tied in for the tail above the butt. This should sweep gracefully upwards in a slow curve.

5 Above the butt, you should now catch in the flat silver tinsel once again and continue to wind this up to the eye.

6 Take a hen hackle dyed pale grey or the shade known as blue dun and strip the fibres from one side. Now tie the hackle in at its thickest end behind the eye and wind it down over the body so that each turn is not too close to each other. Do not remove the hackle pliers just yet.

7 Now take the round silver (the rib) and wind this tightly over the whole of the body in the opposite direction to which the body hackle was wound on so that it passes through the hackle fibres without trapping them down and also secures the hackle in place.

Tie the rib in behind the eye and snip off the remainder.

8 A false hackle of blue jay fibres (or dyed guinea fowl for larger flies) is now tied in at the throat.

9 From a hen pheasant tail, you should now strip out a section that, when folded in half, will be the appropriate size for the wing. Now tie the wing in place so that it lies like that in the drawing (*see* Figure 13).

10 Now we have arrived at the vitally important part – the horns. This can sometimes be difficult and a little practice may be required. A blue macaw tail quill is only blue on the outside, the underside being yellow. Such feathers can sometimes be difficult to obtain but if you are lucky enough to get hold of a good one the fibres will be equal on each side of the stem. Remove a single fibre from each side of the feather.

Looking at the blue side of the feather (the best side), the fibre you remove from the left-hand side will be

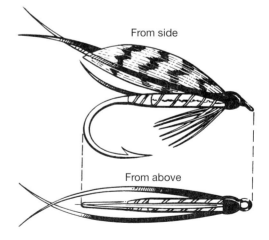

Figure 13. The Haslam, showing the correct position of the horns from the side and from above.

tied in on the right-hand side of the fly, that is the side on the right when looking at the fly with the eye pointing towards you, and vice versa.

The fibres should be twice the length of the hook when tied in. The horns should not be tied to lie over the wing but to circle the outside edge of the wing and cross each other behind it (*see* Figure 13).

Now that you have tied the Haslam you should not have too much trouble in tying the rest of this list of old favourites. Please note that the hooks given for the rest of the dressings in this series are only a recommendation as they can be dressed on a range of wet fly hooks.

ZULU

Hooks	6–12 Kamasan B175
Silk	Black
Tail	Red wool
Body	Black seal fur (or substitute) or black wool
Rib	Silver wire. Oval silver size 14 on larger flies
Hackle	Black, palmered over the body
Wing	None
Head	Black

BLUE ZULU

Hooks	Size 6–12 Kamasan B175
Silk	Black
Tail	Red wool
Body	Flat silver (plain or holographic)
Rib	Silver wire, oval silver size 14 on larger flies

Hackle	Black, palmered over the body
Wing	None
Head	Black

DARK MACKEREL

Hooks	Size 6–12 Kamasan B175
Silk	Black
Tail	Hare guard hairs
Body	Dark claret seal fur or substitute
Rib	Silver wire, oval silver size 14 on larger flies
Hackle	Purple
Wing	Bronze mallard
Head	Black

PETER ROSS

Hooks	Size 6–12 Kamasan B175
Silk	Black
Tail	Golden pheasant tippets
Body	Rear two-thirds, flat silver tinsel (plain or holographic). Upper one-third red seal fur (or substitute)
Rib	Silver wire, oval silver size 14 on larger flies
Hackle	Black
Wing	Teal
Head	Black

SILVER INVICTA

Hooks	Size 6–12 Kamasan B175
Silk	Black
Tail	Golden pheasant crest

Body	Flat silver (plain or holographic)
Rib	Silver wire, oval silver size 14 on larger flies
Hackle	(Body) Palmered natural light red/brown
Hackle	(Throat) Blue jay or dyed blue guinea fowl
Wing	Hen pheasant centre tail
Head	Black

MALLARD AND CLARET

Hooks	Size 6–12 Kamasan B175
Silk	Black
Tail	Golden pheasant tippets
Body	Claret seal fur, or substitute
Rib	Gold wire, oval gold size 14 on larger flies
Hackle	Dyed claret, or black if preferred
Wing	Bronze mallard
Head	Black

A black hackle often works better in the dark.

MALLARD AND SILVER

Hooks	Size 6–12 Kamasan B175
Silk	Black
Tail	Golden pheasant tippets
Body	Flat silver (plain or holographic)
Rib	Silver wire, oval silver size 14 on larger flies
Hackle	Black
Wing	Bronze mallard
Head	Black

BIBIO

Hooks	Size 6–12 Kamasan B175
Silk	Black
Tail	None
Body	Black seal fur, or substitute. Then red seal fur for a short distance in the middle of the body. Then black seal fur again to complete a three-sectioned body
Rib	Silver wire, oval silver size 14 on larger flies
Hackle	Black, palmered over the body
Wing	None
Head	Black

SILVER BIBIO

Hooks	Size 6–12 Kamasan B175
Silk	Black
Tail	None
Body	Flat silver (plain or holographic)
Rib	Silver wire, oval silver size 14 on larger flies
Hackle	Black, palmered over the body
Wing	None
Head	Black

HACKLED SILVER WICKHAM

This one is based on the original Wickham's Fancy.

Hooks	Size 6–12 Kamasan B175
Silk	Brown
Tail	Natural red/brown cock hackle fibres

Body	Flat silver (plain or holographic)
Rib	Gold wire, oval gold size 14 on larger flies
Hackle	(Body) Palmered natural light red/brown
Hackle	(Head) Natural light red/brown wound fully behind head, not as throat hackle
Wing	None
Head	The brown tying silk varnished

Note: If dressed more heavily hackled, some of the above-mentioned flies can be used to 'dibble', that is to skate along the surface as a bob fly.

In larger sizes they can also be used as dapping flies (*see* Chapter 17). The best of the above for this purpose are Zulu, Blue Zulu, Silver Invicta, Bibio, Silver Bibio and Silver Wickham.

ALEXANDRA

Last, but by no means least, in this series is my old favourite on which I caught my very first sea trout. This one was invented around 1860 but it is uncertain who the inventor actually was. It is thought by some historians, however, to have been the invention of W. G. Turle of Newton Stacey. Originally it was called 'The Lady of the Lake', but was renamed in honour of Queen Alexandra.

Hooks	Size 6–12 Kamasan B175
Silk	Black
Tail	Red ibis feather or substitute
Body	Flat silver. In larger sizes ribbed with fine round silver
Hackle	Black hen
Wing	A bunch of peacock sword feather herls with a strip of red ibis on each side
Head	Black. Red is sometimes used in certain areas

A good variation of the Alexandra is the Donegal Alexandra, which features a magenta hackle.

Modern tackle and some old-fashioned flies.

10   Surface Lures

Fishing the surface lure, sometimes referred to as a wake lure, is one of the deadliest methods of catching sea trout. It is so deadly that at least a quarter of all the sea trout I have caught have fell to this.

Quite simply, it is a floating lure that creates a wake when retrieved or hung in the current. There are many variations of this lure, but the ones I have described below are those on which I have caught the most fish, and the ones that I personally have the most confidence in.

The best surface lures are black ones. Earlier, under 'fly lines', I made the point that you should never use a dark-coloured floating line as this is too obvious to a fish looking towards the surface. However, in this case this is exactly what we wish to achieve, and a black lure silhouetted

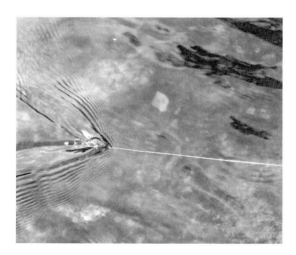

A surface lure in action.

against the night sky will be very obvious indeed, and even more obvious when made to create a wake.

All my surface lures are armed with a trailing treble hook, which takes care of any short-taking fish. A leading hook, situated under the body, not only serves to hook fish, it will also act as a keel to keep the lure swimming upright and prevent it from spinning in the current.

I have tried to catch sea trout on them in the day, but to no avail. I only caught chub and the occasional pike. However, this is a deadly lure in the early part of the night providing it is dark enough. It is also a lure that will often prove too tempting in the dead of night after the fish have gone down. When other types of flies fished on, or close to the surface at this time are not getting much response, this big lure and the disturbance it makes will often, and usually does, provoke an attack.

THE COCKROACH

The materials you will require are:

A piece of hard black foam, which is marketed as Plastazote. Alternatively, you can use an impregnated cork sanding block from your local DIY store, although you may have to colour this later with a black permanent marker.
A size 2 Aberdeen sea hook. The style is not too important just so long as it is not too short in the shank and the eye is large

enough to accommodate the nylon while leaving enough space for the leader to pass through when you come to fish with it. My preferred choice is the straight-eyed P261 BLN Partridge Aberdeen Perfect or the P260 BLN Partridge Pro-Match, which is the same as the Perfect but in finer wire.
A size 14 Partridge outpoint treble hook.
A large black cock hackle.
A length of 10lb WS nylon.
Black tying silk.
A tube of impact adhesive.
Black varnish.
You will also need a sharp craft knife.

The first thing to do is make the mount. These instructions form the basis of mounts you will need in the construction of other lures.

Construction

1   Place the treble hook in the vice, wind on a bed of tying silk and varnish over. Now take the nylon and pass each end through the eye from opposite sides. Now tie the nylon down, varnish over with black varnish and remove from the vice (Figure 14A).
2   Fix the single hook in the vice and wind on a bed of tying silk. Now pass one end of the nylon (which is attached to the treble) through the eye then back on itself. The other end remains pointing forward.

You should now tie the nylon down loosely with three or four turns of the silk so that it is not too tight. This will allow you to adjust the mount to a length that should be 1¾in in total. Once this is achieved, continue to tie the nylon down tightly then snip off the excess ends. Now varnish over with clear varnish but do not remove from the vice (Figure 14B).
3   From the Plastazote (or sanding block) cut a block 1⅛in long by ½in by ½in. Now cut out a V-shaped section about 1⅛in wide lengthways down the centre of the block. Save this piece as it will later be glued back into the main block (Figure 14C).
4   Now run a smear of the impact adhesive inside the V of the main block and over the shank of the hook.

Once the adhesive is almost dry press the main block into place against the upper side of the shank leaving a little space behind the eye (Figure 14D).
5   Once the block is securely glued to the shank, remove the hook from the vice and place it upside down, on its back as it were, on a flat surface. Now run a smear of glue inside the V channel and against two sides of the V. Once the glue is almost dry, press the V section tightly down into the V channel.

Have patience. Do not touch anything until the glue has had time to set properly (Figure 14E).
6   Now you can shape the body using a very sharp pair of scissors. I like to give mine a nice humpback shape. The lure will work best if you leave the underside flat (Figure 14F).
7   Once the lure has been snipped to shape, wind on the black cock hackle

The deadly Cockroach surface lure.

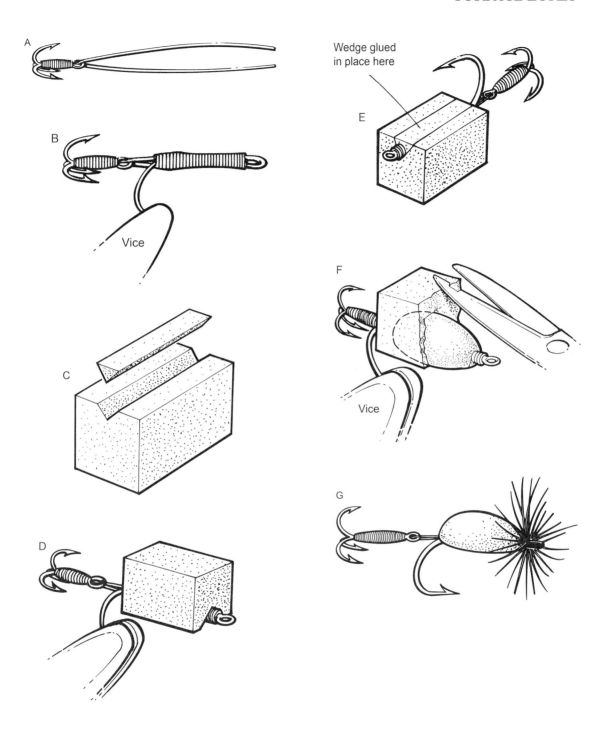

Figure 14. The construction of a mount. See text for instructions.

behind the eye, tie in and complete the head with black varnish (Figure 14G).

THE JIMBO

Working on the theory that sea trout are attracted to lures that have eyes, I also tied up a wake lure that had eyes made from a pair of beads. This also works extremely well, not only for sea trout, but for salmon too. I have sometimes made surface lures with eyes that I simply painted on the underside. In my own experience, surface lures with eyes will attract fish into closer range. My old friend Emelio Mutti and I have taken a good many salmon on the eyed version at night. Who said that salmon don't take a dry fly?

This bead-eyed version, the Jimbo, is similar to the Cockroach except that the black cock hackle is replaced with a pair of pearl beads of about ¼in diameter for eyes, which gives the lure a frog-like appearance. The eyes are easily tied in by threading the beads onto a length of nylon. They are then, with the tying thread, tied in behind the hook's eye with a figure of eight pattern until they are sitting perfectly in place. A drop of super glue over the binding gives added security.

I once joined a small club that has a short stretch of tidal water on a certain stream in

The bead-eyed Jimbo.

the northwest of England. It was here, on a warm and overcast September evening, that I met up with an old friend. Gordon, a likeable bloke with a dry sense of humour, is an old hand on this river and was just the man to show me all the best places to take sea trout. There had, he told me, been plenty of fish entering the river over the past few days and the prospects for a good night's fishing were good. This was what I had been hoping to hear as I had travelled a long way. News like this always triggers that anxious let me get at them feeling and because I hadn't had too much opportunity to fish lately, I was eager to get started.

We set off along the marshy bank, turning the corner where the path lead us through the hazel bushes and over a stile. Now we were looking down a long straight length of water. No exciting pools and rapids, more faster then slacker water and the kind of water that, to the uninitiated, would seem a place to fish for eels rather than sea trout and salmon. But we knew better; game fish did lie here and could be taken once you knew where the lies were. Shades of dusk were fading and the odd sea trout were beginning to make their presence known. Soon they would be plopping all over the river but for now there was time enough for my good friend and I to take a stroll along the river bank.

Gordon pointed out the best lies and recounted some of his greatest fishing experiences here. He told me about the 12lb sea trout that he had caught on a Secret Weapon on a night when the mist was so thick that it was impossible to see the opposite bank. He also told me about the occasion when he hooked a fish so large that it rushed down the river tearing line off the reel until all the backing had gone and the leader was snapped. That had been a good number of years ago and to this day he is left wondering what that fish might have been. He told me about the time he had hooked two 10lb salmon at the same time, one on the point and one on the dropper, and how he had played them for over an hour. This made me think that right now would be a good time of day to fish for salmon, but it was sea trout that I had come for and I was content to share Gordon's good company and listen to his interesting fishing tales.

As the light finally faded into darkness and a warm gentle breeze floated in from the southwest, sea trout began to show in greater numbers and, itching with anticipation, I was more than ready to get cracking. In fact, I was in such a hurry to tackle up that I missed a ring and had to thread up the line all over again. Gordon suggested that I should make my way downstream towards the old footbridge while he went back up the river. This suited me fine as I fancied my chances downstream where the rocky outcrops provided a good sea trout lie.

Using a floating line and a Reuben's Special I cast across the river at forty-five degrees and mended the line so that the current carried the fly to hang squarely under the shrubbery above the rocks. This produced an immediate take from a cheeky little brown trout, giving hope of better things to come. I fished on in the same place for a while until I thought about moving down a little further. But just then I got a good take and lifted the rod into a fish, which began to fight hard. It ran all over the place before it was eventually netted, a lovely fresh sea trout of about 1¾lb, which I carefully returned in the certainty that the next fish would be bigger. Although sea trout continued to show for as far as I could see, I didn't get another offer. After a good hour of hard fishing I decided to move down beyond the bridge.

Perhaps it was also time for a change of fly, and recalling Gordon's tale of the big sea trout on a Secret Weapon this is what I put on. I cast down and across and allowed the fly to gently come round under my bank. It was taken with a hard snatch, which almost took the rod out of my hand. The fish bolted upstream towards me and I had to hand strip the line in as fast as I could go. Next, the fish turned and was heading towards an outcrop of rocks. I applied as much side pressure as I dared. I just had to steer the fish away from those extremely sharp rocks. It didn't work, the fish just kept on going. Fortunately there is a well-trodden path along the bank. I was able to follow it without too much effort and continued the battle with the rod held out at arm's length to keep my fish from burying itself amongst the rocks. By good luck the fish was well hooked and at length I was able to steer it away from danger to a part of the bank that was safe enough to allow me to play it until it eventually glided into the waiting net, a cracking silver sea trout of about 5lb. Most of my fish are returned to the water but this one I decided to keep. Not for myself, but to give to Gordon as a way of saying thank you for the pub meal he had insisted on paying for on the previous occasion we had met.

Funny how time flies when you're fishing. It was now almost midnight and a wave of tiredness had swept over me. The day had been a long and hard one and I felt the need to sit down for a while, and where better than by the old footbridge to which I now made my way. Perhaps Gordon had followed me down and would be fishing close by – I could show him my fish. Perhaps he had caught an even bigger one for himself, but he was nowhere in sight.

I sat in the middle of the bridge with my back against the rusty steelwork and pulled out my flask, hoping that a strong coffee and a Mister Kipling might bring me round. It didn't really work, yet I still felt the urge to fish. It was a case of the mind being willing but the body being knackered.

By this time it might have been more appropriate to fish a Terror or something similar on a sinking line. I looked at the contents of my fly box, thought about trying one of the new patterns that I had recently tied, then changed my mind. It was too much like hard work and besides, in my lethargic state, I didn't feel like changing the line. I simply tied on a Jimbo and dropped it down. I let it play about in the current; you never know, something might come along. Now, with the butt of the rod resting against my leg, it was time to enjoy a smoke and another cup of coffee.

I must have dozed off for the next thing I knew something was twanging against my leg. It took a few moments for me to realise that a fish was hooked and running away with the Jimbo. I grabbed the rod and pulled into a heavy fish that pulled back just as hard. A fight was on. The fish was possessed with anger as it thrashed about in the dark shadow of the bridge, dashing from one side to the other. I fumbled about and eventually found the landing net. But I had to scramble down to the water's edge over a pile of stones that had once been part of the bridge support. Eventually, I stood on what had appeared to be a hard sandy shore but which, in fact, turned out to be sloppy silt that clung like glue to my waders. As the fish fought, I prayed the hook would hold. It did, and after the fish had put up a long and courageous fight, the net was slipped under it. I hauled myself up the bank and away from the mud, which didn't want to let me go. It was a fine fresh fish weighing at least 8lb.

'That was a good fight', came a voice in the dark. I looked up to see Gordon, who had obviously been watching my performance, standing by the side of the bridge. With his usual dry sense of humour he called down, 'What did you get that on then, you lazy bugger?'

I must mention old Jack, who's surname I have omitted for reasons that will become obvious. Jack was not a sea trout fisherman, he didn't even fly fish. He was a coarse fisherman, but even that is an overstatement. He was what is known in the North as a snigger – he just loved catching slimy eels and very little else. So when he asked, or rather pestered, me to take him along on one of my night fishing trips I was reluctant and did all I could to talk him out of it. I even told him that they were serving free beer in the Red Lion, but the old man persisted, promising to keep well out of my way and fish only the 'black hole', which I would not be particularly interested in fishing anyhow. I gave in and arranged to pick him up at his home the following evening.

I turned into the run-down council estate where dogs roam wild and foul the pavement, and toddlers sucking on oversized dummies and wearing grubby vests and nothing else play in the gutter. This was meant to be the council's showpiece when it was built in the mid 1960s, but things had gone downhill since then. I don't suppose it was much different from many other estates across the country. Bike frames and one-wheeled prams now rusted in gardens where they competed for space with the weeds. Pale, hooded, spotty-faced youths

A beautiful 2½lb sea trout taken in early July on a Jimbo.

with hard expressions and red-rimmed eyes loitered on each corner, complaining that they had nothing to do. This wasn't surprising as I had heard that these lads had burned down their own youth club two weeks earlier. Six shops had once served this estate but only one remained, a Co-op, and even that had resorted to steel shutters and a small grill through which cigarettes and booze were passed after cash payment had been made in full.

Then my eye caught sight of something that at first glance appeared like a pile of rubbish that had been tossed into the street. It was only when I got closer that I realised that it was Jack sitting on an old wooden seat box, his scruffy cap, as usual, pulled down over his left eye, his dirty blue and red anorak, three sizes too big, hanging over his knees, while his much patched wellies, still caked in mud from a previous fishing expedition, rested in the gutter. But worse, he was surrounded by buckets and carrier bags full of God knows what, while the tips of battered old rods stuck out of the end of a torn holdall, which most anglers would have long since thrown on the skip. Little chance of Jack getting mugged; you couldn't sell this lot in the pub. How I managed to cram all that fishing junk into the boot of my small car I'll never know. A group of youths were approaching, looking menacingly in my direction. I drew myself up and put on a scowl in an attempt to look big and tough, then breathed a sigh of relief as they swaggered on by, one carrying a plastic bottle with a hole in the side, no doubt intended as a pot-smoking bong. I was glad to get away.

As I drove to the river I would have given anything for a set of ear plugs as, in between scratching unmentionable parts of his body and constantly winding the window down to smoke yet another full-strength fag, Jack went on and on with endless enthusiasm about monstrous eels from some old quarry and the giant lob worms he had dug from a disused sewage farm. As if the conversation wasn't frustrating enough, I kept getting a whiff of something quite obnoxious, which was obviously drifting from the boot. I put my foot down a little harder but by the time we finally arrived on the river bank a mild headache was beginning to develop into something more serious.

I headed upstream as fast as my legs would take me in a pair of chest waders, leaving Jack, now chunnering away to himself, to set out his two snigging rods, a bucket of worms and another bucket of foul-smelling ground bait, which I imagined would give any fish a headache worse than my own.

The night was a glorious one for sea trout fishing. The July sky was cloudy and plenty of fish were showing in the pools. I reached a favourite spot just above where a small brook enters the pool, an excellent spot to fish a surface lure. I put on a Jimbo, on which I had caught sea trout here before, and cast into the meeting of the two currents in the certainty that a sea trout would take, and it did. A beautiful 2lb fish took me right away and fought hard as it dashed here, there and everywhere about the pool, but at last I landed it and returned it carefully to the river. By some strange miracle my headache had now disappeared.

For the next hour or so I didn't catch anything else and was tempted to try another pool. But I resisted the temptation as I had a feeling that a bigger fish was lying here, just biding its time before the lure of the Jimbo passing over it became too much to endure. My patience paid off; suddenly there was a huge swirl and I lifted the rod into a heavy fish that took off at great speed down the pool.

The fish was fairly ripping line off the reel as it headed towards the rapids. I had no choice but to follow it. Down through the white water it went with me in pursuit, scrambling through the rocks along the side. The fish was now thrashing about in the next pool as I crashed through the bracken and forced myself up a slippery bank, but now, at last, I was able to play my big fish with a lesser degree of difficulty. The fish came to the net at least three times, but each time it found yet another reserve of energy and bolted once again into midstream.

The fight eventually reached an end as the fish turned on its side for me to slip the net under it. It was a lovely fish, weighing a little over 4lb. As I admired my prize in the light of my headlamp I heard that unmistakable croaking voice, 'That's a cracker. What did you get it on, Jim?'

Jack was in awe of my fish and obviously my skill; he kept repeating what a good fisherman I must be. I showed him the lure and explained how it worked, while remarking in a tone that, on reflection, must have seemed tainted with conceit, that sea trout fishing beat the hell out of snigging, anytime. This was proper fishing, something only for experts.

'You wouldn't have a spare one, would you?'

'Sorry, it's my last one', I lied, in the hope he would get back to his bootlaces and leave me to get on with some real fishing. I felt sure that he would find it impossible to cast a surface lure with an old fibreglass ledger rod.

Wearing a downcast expression, Jack shuffled off into the night while I resumed fishing. Silly old bugger. But it wasn't long before a feeling of guilt began to set in. Jack must have known that I would have more than a few spare surface lures in my box. And besides, for all his misgivings, he wasn't such a bad old lad, a good-hearted bloke in fact who would give you his last penny, and the shirt off his back if you asked him – even his last worm.

Jack's son and only offspring had emigrated to Australia some fifteen years earlier at the age of twenty three. He had returned once for his mother's funeral three years later. Apart from the cursory Christmas card and the rare phone call there was no other communication. Apparently the son had married out there and was now the father of a ten-year-old son; a grandson who Jack had never seen except on the one blurred photograph that he kept in a tarnished frame hung in pride of place over the mantelpiece. Yet Jack would always tell you what a good lad his son was and how well he was doing as a self-employed builder. If it hurt inside, Jack kept it to himself.

Shortly after his son had emigrated, Jack's wife of thirty years had fell victim to a terminal illness. He had nursed her through to the end with love and tenderness. He was devastated when she finally passed away, even though her passing was an escape from all the pain she had suffered. Jack's eventual comfort, I'm sure, was found in his love of eel fishing. At least it must have helped him through the pain of bereavement.

I wanted to shout him back, perhaps to lie again and say that I had found a spare one, but I didn't have the courage. I felt deeply ashamed. What a snob. How could I have been so mean?

For the next hour I continued to fish but somehow my heart was no longer in it. Perhaps it was fortunate that I had decided to keep the last fish. Perhaps I could now redeem myself by giving it to Jack. Yes, that's what I'd do. He'd like that. Perhaps I'd ease my guilt by buying him a bottle of wine to go with it, or a few bottles of beer if he preferred.

Then suddenly Jack came crashing through the bushes. 'Jim. Jim. Look what I've caught.' I turned, expecting to see the old man proudly presenting his huge eel. But it was no eel that Jack held aloft; it was a big silver sea trout of about 7lb. It was a beautiful fish, a real specimen, fresh up from the sea. Surely no self-respecting sea trout had fallen for one of Jack's stinking lobs. 'No, no, I didn't get it on a worm' he exclaimed as proud as Punch. 'I got it on one of them surface lures.' 'Rubbish! Tell us another one Jack.'

But he had. He had whittled a rough-shaped body from a twig, tied a treble hook to the end of his line and fastened everything together with some insulation tape that he had found in the bottom of his box.

I was astonished and at the same time felt as though I had received a well-deserved smack. But more than that, I had learned a lesson in humility.

'I wouldn't mind taking up this fly fishing lark', declared Jack. 'Dead easy.'

Twelve months after this event, Jack met his grandson for the one and only time as he lay dying in hospital. Two days later he passed away peacefully in his sleep.

A beautiful sea trout pool on the River Dovey at Brigands Inn.

11　The Snake Fly

This is the fly, or rather lure, which no self-respecting sea trout angler should be without. It was designed to represent a sand eel and, having a flexible body, it is extremely life-like when fished against a current. In addition, the flexible body makes it very difficult for a fish to lever off. In smaller sizes, this fly will work in the early part of the night when the fish are near the surface, and equally well in larger sizes as a deep sunk lure in the later part of the night after the fish have gone down. It will take sea trout in the sea, the estuary, and in the higher reaches of the river with equal effect. Since I invented it, it has become one of the most popular sea trout flies in England and Wales and is growing in popularity in Scotland, Ireland and in Scandinavian countries too. The fly has been requested from as far away as the Falkland Islands, Canada and South America. It is not an easy fly to dress; it will take time and patience, but the time taken will, I'm sure, be well rewarded.

After the Snake Fly had been tried and tested and had proved a great success, a description of it was given in my earlier book, *Sea Trout Flies*, published in 1988. Little did I realise at the time just how popular this lure would become. My old friend and professional fly dresser Sid Knight can hardly keep up with the demand. Moreover, I have discovered an Internet site that sells nothing else but Snake Flies. Paul Hopwood, who runs his own sea trout fishing website, informs me that this fly has revolutionised his fishing.

In 1989, a year after the publication of my book, I was fishing a tidal stretch of the River Dwyryd below Maentwrog in North Wales. As I worked a Snake Fly through a likely looking pool it became stuck on the bottom. After tugging away for a while a large twig finally floated to the surface, but what was tangled round it was a big surprise. Not only was there a tangled length of leader on the end of it, but next to my own was another Snake Fly. Even more surprising was the fact that it was exactly the same as my own in every detail, the same colour and even the same length, like two peas in a pod. I might easily have tied it myself and, needless to say, I was flattered.

A few weeks later I was over on the west coast of Ireland. My work was to help promote angling and encourage tourists to an area that had suffered much from the 'troubles'. It was not an easy task. Tourism had all but dried up, but the fishing was as good as ever, especially on lower Lough Erne where I had been more than well looked after by the members of the Enniskillen Fly Fishing Association. I'm sure they will remember me as the twit who managed to get his fly line tangled round the boat's propeller and who managed to lose a huge trout by not taking their advice to use a leader of at least 8lb BS. That was another lesson learned.

During this unforgettable stay, with accommodation second to none at Carlton Cottages in Belleek, I decided one night to cross the border into Ballyshannon to have a go at the sea trout. This is where the River Erne, which drains the great Lough Erne system, enters the estuary. Unfortunately, migratory fish are prevented from running up to the lough due to a high dam in Ballyshannon itself, but this does not prevent them from trying.

When I arrived, two anglers were already fishing below the town bridge so I sat on the bank and watched them for a while. Sea trout were showing in great numbers, yet the two didn't seem to be having much luck. Later, we got round to having a chat, as anglers do, and I was told that the fish were not on the take, their theory being that there were too many sand eels in the estuary on which the sea trout had been gorging themselves. They were giving it up as a hopeless task and about to make for the pub before last orders. I suggested that before dashing off they might like to try one of my Snake Flies and gave them one apiece. 'These look good', said one. 'Might just do the trick.' With that they both tied on a Snake and waded back into the river. One fisherman took a two pounder on the first cast and the other took one a little bigger a few minutes later. I waded in a little further down and in the next hour or so I had five fish to the Snake Fly, the best weighing 3lb, which I was told was an excellent fish for this river.

Funny how word gets round in Ireland. The following day I went to Garrison on the shore of Lough Melvin to visit my old friend Michael Gilroy, who is perhaps the greatest fly fisherman that I have ever had the privilege to fish with. As I walked through the village I was approached by an old character, who asked 'Was it yourself who was in Ballyshannon last night?'

'Why do you ask?' It was wise to exercise some degree of caution in those days.

'I was wondering if it was yourself who gave them Snake Fly things to Sean and John.' I told him I had.

'You wouldn't have any more to spare, would you?'

Naturally, because of this fly's growing use, quite a number of variations have been tied by various fly dressers. Each have their own favourite dressing, but each tell me the same story, that this fly is a must!

The first dressing, or rather instructions, which I have given below, is very similar to the original version. The materials you will need are:

A size 16 or 14 treble hook. (A Partridge X3BL outpoint needle eye is preferred.)
A larger single hook, say size 2 or 4.
A length of slim Mylar, or similar tubing. Do not use tubing that is too fat. The idea is to represent a slim sand eel rather than a fish.
Winging fibres (Optional. See under instruction 8 below.)
A length of 10lb BS nylon.

This lure can be dressed in a range of lengths. For fishing in low water it need not be more than 1½in using a size 16 treble hook. The most popular size is 2½–3in with a size 14 or 12 treble hook. For saltwater fishing it is sometimes dressed up to 5in in length with a treble hook not larger than a size 12.

1   If you are unable to obtain a needle eye treble hook, simply snip off the eye of any suitable treble with a pair of sharp

The original Snake Fly dressing, as first tied in 1985.

snips. This will later help the tubing to slip over easily and avoid a bump above where the tubing is tied down. So we will continue on the assumption that you are not using a needle eye hook (Figure 15A).

2 Fix the treble in the vice. Do not wind on a bed of tying silk as we need to keep the shank as slim as possible to allow the tubing to slip over easily later on. Now take a length of the 10lb nylon between the hooks (Figure 15B).

3 Tie down the nylon, taking care not to catch the hook points with the silk. Apply a drop of super glue or clear varnish, allow it to dry and remove from the vice (Figure 15C).

4 Fix a single hook in the vice. The type matters little but do make sure that the eye is large enough for the nylon to pass through in the process of tying while still leaving enough room for the leader to pass through when you come to fish with it. Now wind on a bed of silk to end a little short of where the hook starts to bend. Thread one end of the nylon through the eye then back on itself. The other end of the nylon lies straight against the shank (Figure 15D). You should now tie the nylon against the shank; not too tight at first so that you can adjust the nylon to the desired length of the lure, which can be from 1 to 4in depending on its intended use.

Once you have adjusted the nylon to achieve the desired length and it is lying straight against the shank, continue to tie the nylon down tightly. Snip off the excess nylon and varnish over with clear varnish or, alternatively, apply super glue.

5 Once the varnish has dried, remove the mount from the vice and snip the hook off below the whipping (Figure 15E).

6 Cut a piece of tubing to the required length. You can use Mylar or any other suitable tubing, as long as it is not too wide. Remember that the idea is to achieve a slim sand eel appearance. I have often used metallic tubing bought from a florist wholesalers, which I found to be excellent. Now place the treble in the vice and slip the tubing over. Apply a little clear varnish to the ends of the tube before slipping it over the mount; this will help to prevent it from fraying (Figure 15F).

7 Tie the tubing down tightly over the treble shank, again taking care not to catch the silk on the treble points. Varnish over with your choice of varnish – red, black or clear will do. Once the varnish has dried, remove the treble from the vice and fix the eye of the leading hook in the vice. This can be a tricky operation that might require a little practice, but more importantly, you will need to ensure that the eye is well clamped.

8 We now need to tie in the 'wing', which should be added sparingly. All we are doing here is giving the lure a little extra movement – a resemblance of life. To overdress would be to defeat the object, as sand eels obviously do not have wings. Tie in the fibres to end just above the points of the treble hook. To tie the fibres beyond this point would cause problems. Firstly, they could tangle round the hooks when casting and cause the Snake to appear somewhat lifeless. Secondly, a sea trout in a tweaking mood would simply nip at the fibre ends and come short of the hook. Do not tie the fibres in on one side, but equally around the body. There are no set rules as to which fibres or colours you should use but bucktail is useful in the longer lures, while squirrel, or

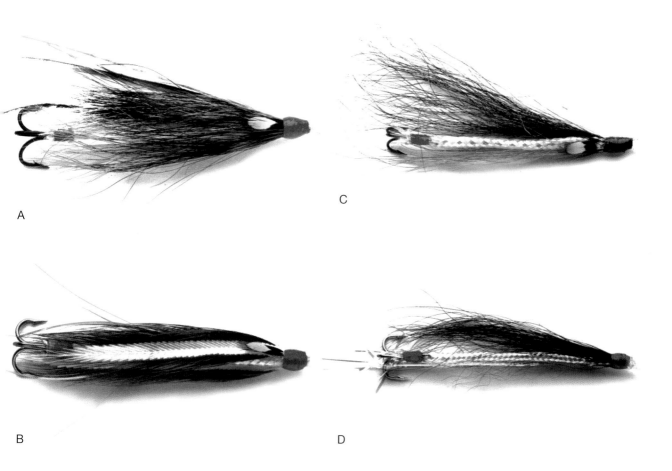

A

C

B

D

Snake Flies. (A) Blue and Squirrel, dressed on a braid mount. (B) An expensive dressing with vulturine guinea fowl feathers as wings. (C) Blue and Silver, dressed on a braid mount using blue goat and natural squirrel tail fibres. This one has a body of phosphorescent Mylar tubing. (D) Black and Orange, dressed on a braid mount using black fox and orange bucktail fibres. (Actual length of each fly is approx. $2^{1}/2$ inches.)

A trio of Snake Flies. (Bottom) A more traditional type of Snake Fly showing its flexibility. (Middle) An unusual Snake Fly dressed with a 'popper' head that will make the fly 'pop' on the surface. (Top) A Snake Fly dressed with a diving vane which gives the impression of a wounded sand eel. (The hand is supplied by John Wilshaw.)

(A, B, C) Three variations of the Alexandra. Note the deadly appearance of the eyed version. (D) Blue Beard. (E) Black Fry. (F) Kerry Gold.

(G) A traditional Medicine, dressed on a Partridge Salar hook. (H) A Gold Medicine, dressed with a bronze mallard wing, a gold tinsel body and a natural red/brown cock hackle. (I) Tammy Troot. (J) Jessica. (K) Joe Pye. (L) Haslam (Sid Knight's dressing).

M

O

N

(M) REF. (N) Dusk. (O) Silent Night. (Dressed by Rosalind Foxon.)

Spectacular scenery, and superb sea trout fishing is to be found along the shore of this sea loch in the northwest of Scotland.

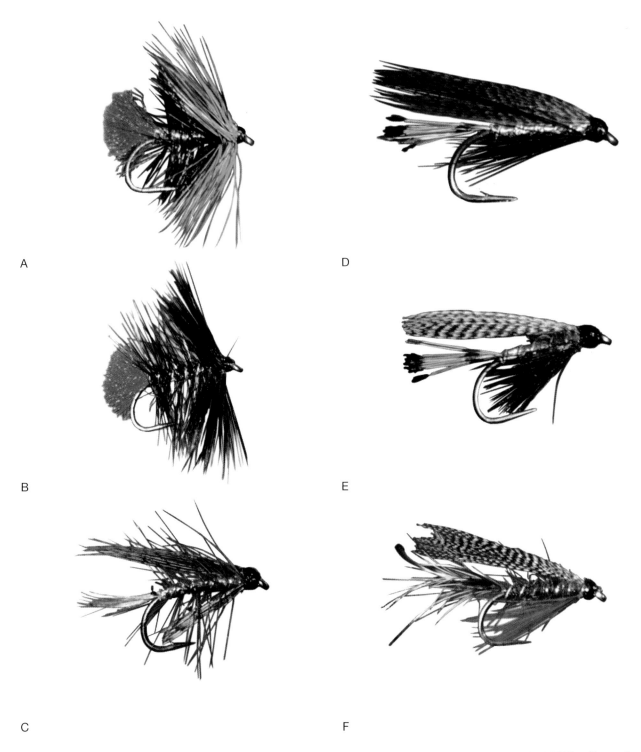

A

B

C

D

E

F

(A) A well-hackled Blue Zulu. (B) A well-hackled Zulu. (C) Hackled Silver Invicta. These first three make ideal dibbling flies, and dapping flies in larger sizes. (D) Mallard and Silver. (E) Peter Ross. (F) Dark Mackerel.

(G) A Blue and Silver Demon. (H) A Blue and Silver Terror. (I) A Black and Silver dressing on a Waddington shank. (J) McHaffie's Secret Weapon. (K) Hoppy's Secret Weapon. (L) Dark Stranger.

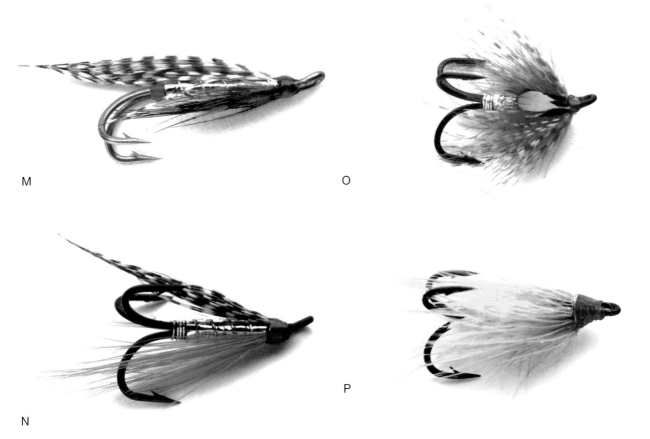

M

O

N

P

(M) A Teal and Blue double. (N) A Teal and Blue treble. (O) The Royal Medicine. (P) The Green Imp.

Dapping flies. Left to right: Blue Zulu, Yellow and Badger, Bi-visible Badger, Badger.

The author making a judged decision. Choosing the right fly for the occasion can so often make the difference between success or failure.

An overcast sky, a good breeze and a good wave. Perfect conditions for dibbling or dapping.

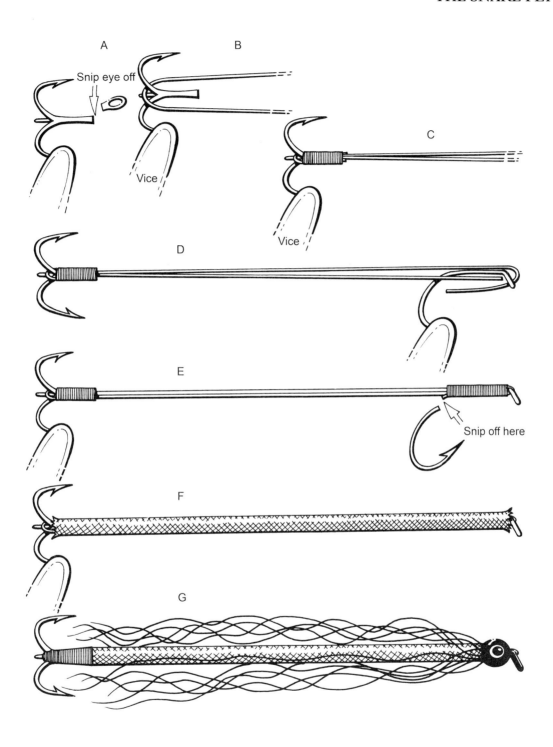

Figure 15. Dressing a Snake Fly. See text for instructions.

similar, is good in shorter ones. If you wish, you can add in a few strands of tinsel fibres to give a little extra flash, but sparingly.

Once you have tied in the wing, continue to wind on the head. Do not try to make a small head as you might in tying a trout fly for instance. A larger head will allow you to paint the eyes on more easily. Now apply a drop of super glue and, once it has dried, varnish with black varnish.

9   Now you can have fun painting on the eyes. To do this it is easier to turn the lure sideways in the vice. The eye is best applied using the point of your dubbing needle, but you will need a steady hand. Alternatively, you could use stick-on eyes, or tie in a pair of jungle-cock eyes (Figure 15G).

This is the original dressing. In more recent years, fly dressers such as Paul Hopwood and Karl Humphries have developed the braid mount version of the Snake. In other words, it is dressed on a mount using braided nylon fly line backing, which is even more flexible. I am grateful to them both for the dressings that they have given me for the production of this book. Paul has provided me with his instructions on how to make a Snake Fly with a braided mount. This is given below.

Tying the Braid Mount Snake Fly
Materials required are:

Braided monofilament backing – 30lb
A darning needle
Super glue
A Partridge needle eye treble hook
Mylar (or similar) tube
Wing material such as bucktail and, if you wish, a few strands of holographic filaments to add that extra something

Construction

1   Cut a length of braided backing to approximately 25 cm.

2   First thread the braid through the eye of the darning needle. Take the needle to one end of the braid leaving about 2 cm of braid at one end. Then thread the braid through the eye of the hook. Feed the hook along the braid so it is near to the needle.

3   Now take the needle and carefully insert it inside the braid on the opposite side of the hook (in doing so you should form a small loop that contains the hook). Thread the needle inside the braid for about 2 cm, then take the needlepoint out of the braid and gently pull the needle through. (This section can be tricky, but gently easing the braid will allow a smoother passage.)

4   Pull the needle clear from the main body of braid; this will also pull the smaller end of braid out. The hook will now be fixed onto the braid by a loop (*see* Figure 16, top).

Remove the needle from the end of the braid and gently smooth the double braid down to the hook. It is important not to exert too much pressure at this point.

5   Cut the small end of braid off very close to the main piece. Once cut, pull the hook so that the cut end of braid pulls itself inside the main part.

6   At this point you can apply a small drop of super glue onto the braid by the hook to give extra strength. You should now be left with a hook attached to a long length of braid.

7   Now re-thread the needle onto the braid (the other end of the mount) and slide the needle along the braid.

8   This section is where the length of the lure is decided. To form the 'eye',

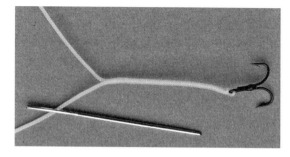

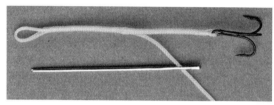

Figure 16. Tying the Braid Mount Snake Fly. See text for instructions.

that is the eye to which your leader is attached, simply thread the needle into the braid towards the hook for a distance of about 2 cm. (Paul usually makes his Snakes about 5–6 cm in length and, in doing this, the ends of the braid meet in the middle of the mount to give added strength, although there is no necessity for this, so longer versions can be tied.)

9 Once you have the desired length, take the point of the needle out through the braid and pull gently to cause a loop to form. Again, it is important not to pull too tight or the loop will disappear into the braid. To prevent this you can place a pen or similar object through the loop which, when formed, should be about 0.5 cm in diameter (*see* Figure 16, middle).

10 Remove the needle and trim off the excess braid as close as possible to the newly formed loop. Do not exert too much pressure until the excess is cut.

Estuaries, such as this one in mid-Wales, are good places to fish a Snake Fly. Sea trout straight from the sea will usually take one readily here.

Once cut, pull the eye slightly until any excess braid disappears inside the sleeve (*see* Figure 16, bottom).

11 Apply a drop of super glue to where the end of the braid lies inside the sleeve. *Do not* apply the glue too close to the eye loop as you will later need to insert a needle into the mount just below the eye. If the braid is stiff at this part it will prevent you from doing so.

12 Fix the eye end of the needle into the vice and push the mount onto the point of the needle just below the eye loop. Cut the tubing to length and slide it down using the point of the needle as a guide. Once the tubing has arrived at the treble hook, tie it down tightly and varnish over.

With the needle still in the vice, tie down the head end of the tubing tightly, as though the needle were a hook, and apply a drop of super glue.

13 Now you can tie in the winging material as in the original version. Again, apply a drop of super glue and, once it has dried, continue to form the head with the silk. Apply varnish over and paint on the eyes which no Snake Fly is complete without. You can now remove the needle.

Added action
Here are two simple ideas that will give the lure even more action, although the concept is nothing new. Quite simply, we are transforming the lure into a plug that will cause it to dive and weave to imitate a wounded fish; and we might do well to bear in mind that there is nothing so attractive to a predator than its wounded prey.

1 From a sheet of clear, stiff plastic, cut a teardrop shape 1in long by ¾in wide tapering to a fine point. Drill a hole just large enough for the eye of the hook to pass through close to the pointed end (Figure 17A).

2 Push the eye through the hole in the teardrop and tie down the point of the teardrop (which is on top of the hook's shank). Continue with the silk to form the head. A drop of super glue is required to secure things in place. Warm the teardrop and squeeze it between your finger and thumb until it becomes slightly bent, forming a shallow spoon (Figure 17B). By bending the teardrop downwards, you can vary the lure's mode of action.

It is a good idea to make a number of different lures with the teardrop bent down at various angles to suit whatever action you wish the lure to have.

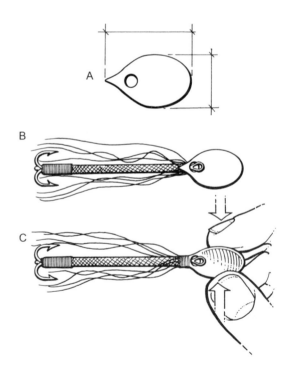

Figure 17. Giving the lure added action. See text for instructions.

The Snake Fly, with the vane attached, will swim with an erratic action which appears like a wounded sand eel.

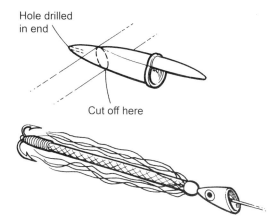

Figure 18. Using a ballpoint pen cap to add action. See text for instructions.

A Snake Fly dressed with a 'Popper' head.

Another easy way to add action is to use the cap from a cheap ballpoint pen.

Simply cut the cap at an angle and drill a small hole in the end. All you then have to do is slip the cap over your leader before tying on the fly. It does not matter that the cap is not tied down. As long as it sits touching the eye of the fly it will still give it all the action it needs. It can be a good idea to paint or stick eyes on the cap itself.

Another good and simple way to add action to your Snake Fly is to dress the body slightly shorter, to end a little distance behind the head, and glue on a 'Popper' head. These are pre-shaped in the form of a cone, with a concaved face and slotted bodies made from a high-density foam. They are easy to fit and are available from most game fishing suppliers. All you need to do is to apply impact glue inside the slot and push the popper head into position. Once the impact glue has almost dried, squeeze the popper head so that it glues everything tightly together. You can now paint it with acrylic paint. The one shown in the photograph is dressed with gold Mylar tubing, a wing of silver Lure-flash and a bright-red cock hackle behind the head, which is painted bright red and features eyes. Snakes that are dressed in this way will swim in an erratic manner and 'pop' across the surface. They also make good pike lures.

In August 2005 I noticed on a certain website that someone had claimed that an angler with a very similar name to my own was the actual inventor of the Snake Fly. Well, I don't suppose that there is anything new in the world of fly dressing and it might just be possible that someone before me did dress a similar lure. All I can say is that I distinctly remember the day in 1985 that I devised the Snake, and that I had never seen or heard of a similar lure to it before that, not even within the pages of my extensive library of game fishing books. I can also remember writing about it in a well-known game fishing publication shortly after I had dressed it. Also, as mentioned earlier, a description of it was given in a previous book that I wrote. I am reminded of the night when I was enjoying a pint in a remote moorland pub on quiz night. The question was asked, 'Who wrote the musical, West Side Story?' An old farmer, who was obviously the worse for drink, put his hand up. 'I know that', he slurred. 'Aye, that's him. Albert Einstein.'

'Near enough, Ted', said the quizmaster, and awarded him a point.

A 3lb sea trout taken on a Snake Fly from the lower reaches of the Cumbrian Leven. This fish was taken as the level was falling with the ebbing tide.

12   Beating the Tweakers

The tweaking sea trout phenomenon is something we all encounter from time to time. The fish simply nip the end of the fly, and sometimes the middle of it, without ever coming into contact with the hook. This is quite an amazing feat when you think that the crafty fish has darted in on the fly, examined it and gone at almost the speed of light – and in the dark too! I have hardly known a night when at least one sea trout didn't nip the fly; that sudden tug, and nothing hooked. Why this should oc-cur is difficult to say, but you will get many more tweakers when rain or thunder is due. This chapter will deal with fish in such a mood and look at some patterns designed to beat them. But first …

Many years ago I lived in Troon in Ayr-shire and was able to fish such rivers as the Ayr, the Doon, and the Girvan, amongst others. But it was the much under-rated River Ayr that I had a particular love affair with. At Stair the river offers exciting sea trout fishing on some of the most beautiful water you ever did see, and it was here that my interest in defeating the short takers was kindled.

Looking back at the notes in one of my old diaries I am reminded of a day, or rather day and night, in mid July. Weath-erwise it had been a day of contrasts. First breezy then calm, cloudy then bright, warm and then cool, wet and then dry, and now that the sun had gone down the tempera-ture had dropped with it and the sky had become as black as a coal miner's under-pants and was threatening to chuck it down.

But here I was, alone on the bank of the River Ayr with plenty of sea trout splashing in the pools but as yet none hooked. This was not to say there was no interest. There had been plenty, but all had been tweakers and teasers nipping away at the fly without becoming hooked. This is not uncommon to us sea trout anglers. There are nights like this when the fish can drive you insane. By about 11pm I had changed the fly quite a number of times but none had worked. The only fly I had not tried was a small low-water salmon fly dressed short on a fine wire Wilson hook. I didn't really think it would work, but nothing ventured, nothing gained, so I tied it on and within the next hour I had caught three good sea trout on it.

The tweakers had been fooled – at least on this occasion. It did, however, occur to me that the body of this fly had been dressed above the point of the hook, so it made sense to assume that sea trout intent on tweaking had honed in on the silver tag at the end of a black body. I guessed, and was probably right as subsequent experi-ments have proved, that the silver tag pro-vided a 'target' area for a tweaking fish to nip at and consequently find itself hooked.

It was after this fishing session that my interest in combating sea trout in this mood grew and with it the range of flies in my collection. Some are described as Secret Weapons, of which similar patterns have been written about in other works. The ones that I write about here, however, are the ones that I have the most confidence in

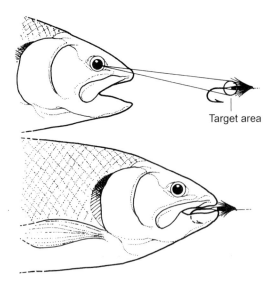

Target area

Figure 19. The silver tag at the base of this short-dressed fly provides a target area for the tweaking sea trout to nip at.

and the ones that I am sure you will catch the most fish on. Here are the dressings for two useful short-dressed flies.

Short-dressed pattern no. 1

Hooks	6, 8 or 10 Partridge CS17 extra long Limerick streamer hooks
Silk	Black
Tag	Phosphorescent tape (the 'target') starting just above the point of the hook
Body	Black silk floss over upper half beyond point of hook
Rib	Silver wire
Hackle	Black cock
Wing	Black squirrel tail fibres
Head	Black (eyes optional)

Note: The tag of phosphorescent tape will glow for some time after being held under the light of your torch and will serve to make the 'target' area more identifiable for any short-taking fish to aim at.

Short-dressed pattern no. 2

This one is dressed on a long shank hook and is ideal when a slightly heavier fly is required.

Hooks	Size 4, 6 or 8 Partridge D4AF bucktail streamer hooks
Silk	Red
Body	The lower half is silver holographic tinsel. The upper half is red seal's fur. Again, the body is dressed over the upper half only beyond the hook's point
Rib	Fine round silver
Hackle	Natural red cock hackle
Wing	None
Head	Red. This has yellow eyes with black centres

A further development in the war against tweaking fish was the Secret Weapon. This is a fly that is constructed with a single leading hook and a small treble closely behind. The original concept, however, was a fly that would present a tasty offering of maggots on the leading hook so that when the crafty sea trout attempted to nip at them it found itself hooked on the treble. This leads us in to a debate on which I promise to be brief.

Using maggots on a fly at night is nothing new and it can be a deadly method of taking fish during the first few hours of darkness. It will even produce results when fished deep and slow later in the night when the fish are taking a rest from their initial burst of activity and are too lethargic to chase a fast-moving lure. At this time maggots can often be too much of a temptation.

There are some, particularly those who were brought up on coarse fishing, who believe that maggots are the answer to everything, but this is not always the case in catching the unpredictable sea trout. I have known nights when the combination of maggot and fly has proved a winner but, equally, I have known just as many occasions when the fish would not touch a fly that had maggots attached. Such are the moods of this fish. On some waters, the use of maggots is completely banned in the belief, rightly or wrongly, that they are unsporting. Personally, I have no argument with their use in conjunction with a fly. As far as I'm concerned, it is just one more method of taking sea trout. More recently, I heard of a club that was considering banning Snake Flies because they were considered too deadly. This makes me wonder where it will all end. If anglers were to turn up on a game water armed with buckets full of maggots and swim feeders, that would be a different matter. It is not so much the method the angler uses, it is his skill in playing the fish and his sportsmanship that is important. Having said all that, I can't remember when I last used maggots on a fly. I seem to catch enough sea trout without them. For me, they're just too much trouble, especially at night. I hardly know anyone who uses maggots who, at one time or another, hasn't had some dreadful experience with them. I even know an angler whose wife made him sell the family car after the lid had come off his bait tub. He tried to scoop them up but they kept appearing. In desperation he doused everything with insect killer, bee killer, bleach and anything else he could lay his hands

on, but they were still crawling all over it. Not to mention the smell, which was worse than the smell of the maggots and which he then tried to disguise with all manner of air fresheners, aftershave and perfumes, which turned out to be even harder to get rid of.

I remember the time, as a young lad, when I set off on the bus to fish a lake some twenty miles from home. It was a hot day when I boarded the bus and took my seat upstairs. I paid the conductor for a return journey then sat back to enjoy the view and think about all the fish that I was going to catch. About halfway there I looked down and was shocked to see thousands of maggots crawling all over the floor. I got off at the next stop, telling the conductor, who looked like a man not to be messed with, that I had suddenly thought of a better place to fish.

If you would like to try using them, you should bear in mind that maggots are not easy to cast with a fly rod and have a tendency to flirt off if the cast is too hard. You will need to develop a soft, rounded casting action and be accurate with it, which is not always easy, especially in the dark.

It would be a misconception if you thought that the Secret Weapon type of fly was only useful if there were maggots attached. Nothing could be further from the truth. A good dressing of this fly can be extremely attractive to sea trout, not to mention the excellent hooking potential.

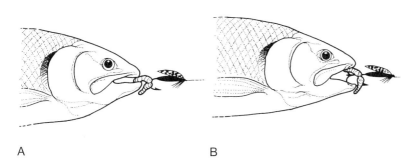

A   B

Figure 20. (A) A tweaking sea trout nips at the maggots and eludes the leading hook. (B) But he will be hooked by a small treble set astern.

This first Secret Weapon dressing is one of my own on which I have caught countless sea trout over the years. It is a somewhat scruffy-looking fly but nevertheless deadly.

The dressing

Hooks	Treble, size 16 standard treble hook. Leading hook, size Partridge YL2A Captain Hamilton
Silk	Red
Body	(Leading hook only) A mixed dubbing of reddish-brown seal's fur (or substitute) and grey rabbit fur
Rib	Copper wire
Hackle	A natural red hen hackle
Wing	Bronze mallard
Head	Red
Length	1¼in

Construction

Note: Similar instructions for making lure mounts are found elsewhere in this book. They are included again here so that you can follow the complete process without referring to other pages when dressing this particular fly.

1   Fix the treble hook in the vice and wind on a bed of tying silk.
2   Loop a short length of 10lb nylon round the treble and bring both ends out through the eye from opposite sides. Whip the nylon to the shank of the treble and then whip the strands of nylon together above the eye of the treble.
3   Varnish over the whippings with red varnish. Remove the treble from the vice and lay to one side while the varnish dries.
4   Fix the leading hook in the vice and wind on a bed of tying silk.
5   Bring one strand of the nylon (that attached to the treble) through the eye of the hook and back along the shank. Cut off the other strand below the eye of the hook (Figure 21A).
6   Tie down the nylon mount to the hook shank taking care to maintain equal tension in the two strands. It should be well tied down to prevent the risk of stripping away should a big fish take hold (Figure 21B).
7   Tie in a short length of the copper wire at the bend of the hook, which will later form the ribbing.
8   From the bend wind on the body dubbing, which is an equal mix of reddish-

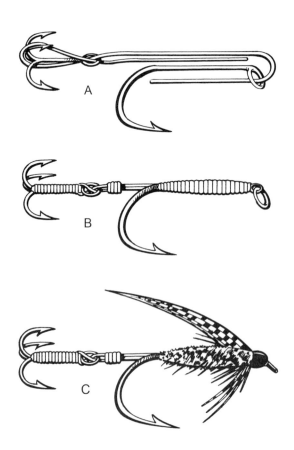

Figure 21. Dressing Jim's Secret Weapon. See text for instructions.

brown seal's fur and the grey under-fur from a rabbit.

9 Wind on the copper wire (about five or six turns) over the body for the ribbing, which will help to protect the soft dubbed body from the sharp teeth of a sea trout.

10 For the hackle, wind on three or four turns of the red hen hackle, which is then fluffed out.

11 Tie in a sparse wing of bronze mallard, which should end level, or just short, of the eye of the treble.

12 Continue to wind on the tying silk to complete the head, which should then be varnished with red varnish (Figure 21C).

You do not need to be too precise about the dressing of this one – the intention is to create a scruffy-looking creature.

McHAFFIE'S SECRET WEAPON

This 'secret' pattern was created by Robert McHaffie of Limavady following a conver-

McHaffie's Secret Weapon.

sation regarding the virtues of such 'secret'-type patterns in general. I liked the look of this and couldn't wait to try it. It has subsequently proved an amazing catcher of sea trout – with or without maggots. Robert made no attempt to disguise the treble hook, just the opposite in fact, and has dressed the treble hook with fluorescent red tape. Although the intention of a Secret Weapon is to hook the fish on the treble when it comes to nip at the main body of the fly, it is still a fly I would not like to be without on occasions. You can, if you wish, choose to apply black varnish to the whipping of the treble. I also think that the killing potential of this one is increased with the addition of eyes.

The dressing

Hooks	Treble hook, size 16. Leading hook, size 8 Captain Hamilton
Silk	Red
Body	(Treble hook) Fluorescent red tape, or alternatively paint over the tying silk with fluorescent red paint or varnish
Body	(Leading hook) Light brown floss silk
Rib	Fine gold wire
Hackle	A cock hackle dyed crimson
Wing	Bronze mallard
Head	Black with yellow eyes
Length	$^7/_8$–1in

Note: An alternative body of gold wire varnished over and not ribbed can be used when the fly is required to fish a little deeper.

DARK STRANGER

This Secret Weapon will be hard to beat. It is a beauty of a dressing that was given to me some time ago when fishing in North

Wales. Unfortunately, it was a dark night and I was tired. Consequently, I forgot to ask my fellow angler his name and I'm not even sure that I would recognise him again, but with a bit of luck he might read this book some day and get in touch with me. I would like to thank him for his kindness and for the excellent sport I have had on his fly. It is a real good looker, which is sure to trigger the three factors of curiosity, aggression and the instinct to feed. For the above reasons, I have taken the liberty of calling this one The Dark Stranger.

The dressing

Hooks	Treble, size 12 Partridge standard treble hook. Leading hook, size 8 single Wilson
Silks	Black and red
Body	(Treble hook) This is not so much a body but the whipping, which is black, then red, then black again
Body	(Leading hook) First a short butt of the black tying silk. Then a short tag of the red tying silk. Then again the black tying silk wound up to the eye to complete the body. The entire body is varnished over with clear varnish
Hackle	Soft black hen hackle with just a few white hen fibres tied in closer to the head
Wing	Two matching black cock hackles tied in side by side with two or three strands of pearl Krystal Flash over
Cheeks	Jungle cock
Head	Black
Length	1¾in

Note: The treble is a little further away from the leading hook than the first Secret Weapon dressing. This is because there was never any intention to impale maggots to the leading hook. Nevertheless, the trailing treble deals well with any fish intent on tweaking.

HOPPY'S SECRET WEAPON

This Secret Weapon was given to me by Paul Hopwood. Paul has a particular liking for this one, which sports a treble that is even further away from the leading hook than the last one. He has taken a lot of sea trout on it, especially on the River Teifi, where he is something of a regular. Paul's fly had no particular name so for convenience I have called it Hoppy's Secret Weapon. It is a difficult one to dress, but I'm sure your efforts will be worthwhile. I never could determine whether this one came under the heading of Secret Weapon or Demon. Perhaps it lies somewhere inbetween. I have a feeling that the luminous bead above the treble hook plays some part in this lure's success.

Personally, I have found this not only useful at night but also in the day when fishing on lower tidal beats. Not long after coming into possession of this fly, I took a fine 4lb sea trout on the estuary of the River Fowey below Lostwithiel.

The dressing

Hooks	Treble, size 8 Partridge X3BL tube fly treble. Leading hook, size 5 Partridge Salar (silver finish)

Note: Partridge Salar hooks are often given in odd sizes from 3 to 11. The tube fly treble has an oval needle eye that is pushed and then glued into the bead (*see* Body).

Silk	Red
Body	(Treble hook) Of red tying silk

varnished over with a small luminous or phosphorescent bead at the eye. This bead, which glows in the dark, makes a good 'target' for nipping fish to aim for

Body	(Leading hook) Silver holographic tinsel
Rib	Fine round silver
Hackle	Guinea fowl dyed red
Wing	Black squirrel tail fibres with a few strands of pearl Krystal Flash mixed in
Head	Red
Length	2½in

Note: The mount is made from fine pike wire with fine clear plastic tube over, separating the two hooks, which should be about 1¼in apart.

Dawn on a Highland spate river. Plenty of water and plenty of fish here.

13 Fishing Deep

On those nights when all the activity has only lasted for the first two or three hours and the fish are now lying on the bottom, the time has arrived to consider a change in tactics. I must again emphasise here that not all nights divide in such a way. I have fished on countless occasions when there was no early activity whatsoever. I speak only in general terms, but now, in what is called the second half, it is time to put on a lure designed to fish deep using a suitable sinking line that will take it to where the fish are now stationed. If you are fishing a fast, deep pool then a high-density line might be needed. Alternatively, where the river is flowing at a more gentle pace, a slower sinking line might be more appropriate. On other pools where the flow is slow and shallower an intermediate line might do the trick. But whatever line is called for, the aim is to get the lure to swim close to the bottom. I would, however, advise against the use of a sink tip line at night unless you are well practised in its use. If you didn't know, a sink tip is a floating line, which graduates into a sinking line for the last few yards. There are a few occasions when I use a sink tip line, but I should point out that they are not as easy to cast as other lines and that the chances of a tangle or the line landing less gently than you would wish are considerably increased – especially in the dark.

The lures for this purpose are often referred to as 'sunk lures', but such a description might be confusing because all lures, with the exception of the surface lure, are expected to sink to some degree. For clarification it is probably better to refer to them as 'deep sunk lures'. Such lures should be fished as slowly as possible. A lethargic sea trout in a state of semi-sleep will not be inclined to use up precious energy by chasing after something moving too fast. As I have mentioned earlier, the lure will be attacked when it invades, or is considered to be competing for, the sea trout's self-allotted space. This is one reason why the lure should not be too small. A small or fast-moving lure, which appears as a tiddler making its way up the river, might not be considered too much of a threat. These are two good reasons why this lure should be fished very slowly. There is a third reason why I think the lure is likely to be attacked and this is linked to the curiosity factor, which is why some patterns seem to work much better than others. In simple terms, I think that if I were a sea trout trying to take a rest and a deep sunk lure came by me, I might be inclined to give it a nip to tell it to clear off. And, in addition, if the dressing was such that by its 'abstract' appearance I was unsure just what it was I might

A typical 'Terror' hare. This one is dressed with a tuft of red wool as a tail on each hook.

also be inclined to take a bite just to satisfy my curiosity. For this reason there is much scope here for the fly dresser to be inventive.

To achieve the desired length and weight, deep sunk lures are best dressed on hooks mounted in tandem with a good distance between each hook. The reason for this is that in almost every case, although there will always be exceptions to the rule, a sea trout will be hooked on the 'tail' hook. However, the leading hook can often serve a useful purpose: when a fish is hooked and turns to run the leading hook will often secure a second hold under the fish's jaw (*see* Figure 22) and should the 'tail' hook

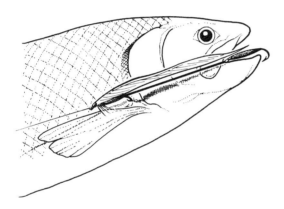

Figure 22. Here the tail hook has torn away from the fish's mouth but the leading hook has secured a hold in the side of the fish.

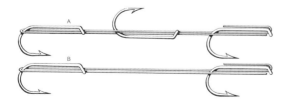

Figure 23. The mount construction of (A) a Terror with three hooks, and the construction of (B) a Demon with two hooks.

tear away, which is not unusual when a big fish is hooked, the leading hook continues to hold the fish. For this reason it might be more advantageous to use a double as the leading hook; being angled outwards it has an increased chance of hooking into the fish, unlike a single hook that might be more inclined to lie flat against the fish without hooking in. A further advantage to using a double leading hook is that it will keep the lure swimming on a more even keel. But on the other hand, a lure dressed on single hooks will usually get more attention because it swims with a lighter, fluttering action, which is more attractive.

Most deep sunk lures are listed as Terrors and Demons, but here some confusion arises as to which type of lure is which. This is because over time some writers have described a particular lure as a Terror while others have described the same lure as a Demon. For clarification I offer the following definitions:

Terror   A lure that has more than two hooks of any kind in tandem. More often a Terror has three hooks; the leading and tail hook down and the middle hook up.

Demon   A lure that has two hooks of any kind (usually single or double) tied in tandem.

These lures are not only useful late at night, they can also be deadly in estuarine waters and even the sea, especially when the sea trout are, or have recently been, feeding on sand eels. I remember watching a young boy take a 10lb sea trout on a Blue Terror from a jetty on the shore of Loch Long while mackerel fishing. They also have their use in heavy and coloured water when the river is running off following a spate. I have taken many sea trout on them in these conditions. They can also work well in a clear spate. This is when the river is in spate yet running clear without being stained by peat or soil, which is often the case when the river runs through a rocky landscape rather than through peat moors or a lowland valley. The Cumbrian Esk is one river that comes to mind. I have experienced high and clear water on this river when such a pattern was put to good use – not only for sea trout but for salmon too.

One of the most successful sunk lures is one that was designed by the late Hugh Falcus. It is a Demon pattern, which makes use of the much-tried combination of blue and silver.

The dressing

Hooks	Two size 8 medium shank hooks. Alternatively, use a size 6, R1A Partridge double Limerick as the leading hook
Silk	Red
Body	(Both hooks) Silver tinsel. The silver holographic tinsel is recommended
Wing	Two cock hackles dyed 'teal' blue with a few strands of bronze peacock herl tied in to rest over the hackle feathers
Head	Red. Usually the red head is given to the leading hook only
Length	2½–3in

Construction

1 Fix the hook (the tail hook) in the vice and wind on a bed of the tying silk from the eye to a point opposite the hook's point.

2 Loop a short length of 15–18lb BS nylon and bring both ends out through the eye (Figure 24A).
Note: The breaking strain of nylon given is only a guideline. Much will depend on the length of the lure and the weight of the tail hook. It should, however, be thick enough to prevent the tail hook from drooping. I have tied these lures in sizes from 2 to 6in long but the average size of this type of lure is 2½in.

3 Whip the nylon tightly to the shank. It is important that it is well tied down as a big fish is capable of stripping the hook from the shank of a poorly tied lure (Figure 24B).

4 Varnish over the whipping with clear varnish. Before the varnish has dried, catch in a short length of medium flat silver tinsel and wind this to the eye. Tie in and snip off the remainder. The varnish will glue the tinsel down as it dries.

5 Once the varnish has dried, remove the tail hook from the vice and lay to one side. Place the leading hook in the vice (single or double) and wind on a bed of tying silk as before.

6 Take up the mounted tail hook and bring one strand of the nylon through the eye of the leading hook and back along the shank until the desired length of the lure is achieved (*see* Figure 24C). Snip off the other strand below the eye of the hook and tie everything down firmly.

7 As before, varnish over the whipping, catch in the silver tinsel and wind this to the eye. Tie in and snip off the remainder.

8 The nylon strands linking the two hooks are now whipped together. This can be a tricky operation, but the easiest way is to fix the two hooks in opposite vices while ensuring that the mount is taut and that the hooks are in line. You can now bind the strands with ease (*see* Figure 24D). Once you have whipped the strands together you can then varnish over with black varnish.

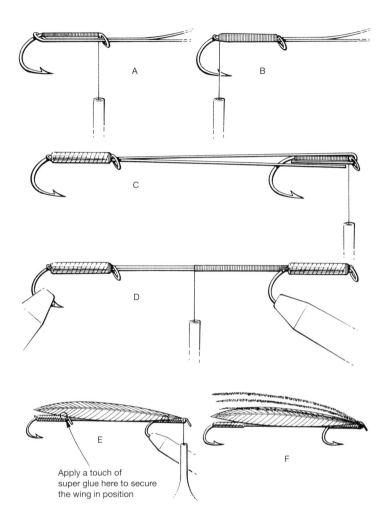

Apply a touch of
super glue here to secure
the wing in position

*Figure 24. The construction of
a Demon pattern. See text for
instructions.*

9 For the wing, tie in two light-blue cock hackle feathers. (The shade known to fly dressers as 'teal' blue is best.) These should lie side by side and end level with the point of the tail hook. Should the wing be too long it is likely to be nipped by tweaking fish that fail to take beyond the point of the hook. Moreover, a wing that is too long is also likely to turn under the mount when casting and be held in this position by the tail hook, which will prevent the lure from swimming correctly.

To keep the hackles in their true position it is advised to apply a drop of super glue to the head of the tail hook and allow the fibre tips to lightly touch down on the glue until it has dried (Figure 24E).

10 Tie in a few bronze peacock herls to rest over the hackles. Snip off the roots and continue to wind on the silk to form the head (Figure 24F).

11 The lure is completed by applying red varnish to the head.

THE GOGGLE EYED DEMON

The next Demon is one of my own inventions. It features eyes that, I think, increase the sea trout's interest.

This particular lure is the one on which I tempted a massive sea trout from the River Fowey (pronounced 'foy' for joy) in Cornwall. It was at the end of August on a night when one would have expected to find the river full of fish. Three days earlier it had rained hard and raised the river by a good foot or so. But it had run off quickly and was now clear and almost back to its normal summer level. What more could a fisherman ask for? The answer is obvious – fish! In the light of the day I walked at least two miles of bank without seeing so much as a minnow. Nothing, although this wouldn't be the first time I had walked a river without seeing any sign of fish. But this time, unfortunately, I just had a gut feeling that the river was empty.

I was on holiday and had been given leave from my long-suffering wife to go sea trouting, so I had to make the most of it. It wasn't like being back home when, if the river wasn't on form, I could easily try again the following night. Besides, I really wanted to catch a Fowey sea trout. I deceived myself that the fish must be hiding in places where my polaroids couldn't penetrate.

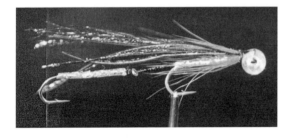

The Goggle Eyed Demon. This ridiculous-looking lure is similar to the one on which I hooked, and lost, a big River Fowey sea trout.

The Lanhydrock Estate water is not the easiest to fish. For the most part its banks are overhung with trees and, although it is truly a beautiful and interesting stretch of river, there are few pools that offer a good casting opportunity. Most of it is only fishable, on the fly at least, by wading down the middle of the river and hoping that the trees can be avoided in the dark. If I were only four feet tall and fished with a five-foot rod I would have few problems fishing here. But circumstances such as these should be seen as an opportunity to improve ones skills, not as an opportunity to moan – so I just got on with it.

As the sun's red embers kindled in the sky, I passed through the fishermen's gate and walked along the narrow carriageway that leads to the ornamental bridge beyond which is Bodmin Park railway station, perhaps the most picturesque, and probably the most photographed, railway station in the world. I crossed the bridge, passed through the small iron gate, then made my way down the track, which lead me to a glorious pool under the bridge. I studied this pool for the second time that day. Surely there had to be a fish or two lying in the deeper run against the wall, but any cast under the bridge would have to be made with some degree of accuracy. It was tempting to have a cast there and then, but I decided that it was still just a little too light. Instead I made yet another mental note of how I would later approach this pool in the dark and continued down the river to a lower pool, which I had noted was not quite so difficult to get a line across.

This lower pool must be one of the most exciting and 'fishy'-looking pools that you will ever see. At its head, white water rushes through a narrow channel, then widens out into what might be considered a great salmon pool. Halfway down the pool the bottom drops over a ledge into deeper water to form what might be described as a double pool. From the tail of the pool the river turns sharply to the right, offering another good lie under a high bank before running straight for about two-hundred yards towards the next bend. Surely I had misread the river. There just had to be fish here. But on a night like this they should have been showing by now – none were.

I fished that pool with intensity, covering every inch of it. I tried every fly I thought might work until, by midnight, I was convinced that my initial instinct had been correct – the river was without fish. I thought about giving up. Perhaps I would have a cast or two under the bridge on my way back. But just then there was one almighty splash at the tail of the pool. It was such a loud splash that at first I didn't think it could have been a fish. I nervously strained my eyes into the darkness to see what lout had tossed a rock into the water. But who, at this time of night, would come all the way out here in these spooky woods to throw a rock into the river? It crashed again and this time I saw it clearly. From experience, I knew it was not a salmon but a big sea trout.

I thought wrongly that the big fish, which must surely have been in double figures, might take a surface lure – it didn't. If a fish wants a surface lure it won't waste too much time in having a go at one, but after a half hour or so and no interest shown I considered that the fish must be well on the bottom, or perhaps it had run upstream. My senses told me that it hadn't; it was here close to where it had crashed. If the fish had gone down for the night it was perhaps wiser to fish deep and slow, so I changed to a sinking line and put on a silver and blue Demon.

I must have fished the Demon over that fish a hundred times or more but it was having none of it. How ungrateful, I thought. I had gone to a lot of trouble to dress that lure. Now it was time to try

something else. I turned my back to the water, switched on my little torch and took a good look in my fly box. Too many to choose from. I should not have brought this big box out, but when you're on holiday… I knew that my choice would have to be from the selection of deep sunk lures, but which one? An eyed Demon stood out, but hadn't I always claimed that the addition of eyes increased the fish's interest. This one, however, had caught my eye not because it was such a good dressing, nor because it had worked so well in the past, but because it looked a bit of an odd ball against the others, a rather bizarre lure that I had dressed as a whim more than anything else. I had looked at it on a number of occasions in the past, thought about using it, then changed my mind on the grounds that such an ugly thing could never work so well as the others. But perhaps this solitary fish might go for something more ridiculous. Something that might annoy it more than anything else. It was worth a try, so with nothing to lose I tied it on. Now the litmus test.

I chanced wading a little further down the pool while trying to remember where the river bed dropped off. I cast as far as I could to the tail of the pool, gave the line a few seconds to sink, and began to retrieve very slowly.

The take was not fierce, as I might have expected from such a big fish. It was more of a slow pull, but as I lifted the rod the fish took off like something possessed, tearing line off the reel as it dashed out of the pool and round the bend and into the long straight. It was a powerful fish and I had no chance of slowing it, not yet at least. I just had to let it run. The problem now was that the line was now rubbing against the tree roots on the comer of the opposite bank as the fish continued on its way down the straight. To get a direct line on it meant that I would have to wade even further down the pool, something that I was very uneasy about, knowing that not too far ahead of me the river bed dropped over the ledge that I had noted earlier. I inched my way forward with the pool getting deeper and deeper. I knew the ledge was somewhere just ahead of me but the line was still running against the roots on the far corner. Just a little further, then a little bit further still, but it was too late. I was sliding over the ledge into deep water, so deep that you might say I was up to my neck in it; well at least my shoulders. My life flashed before me. I dug my heels in and tried to back peddle, but with the weight of the water pushing me forward it was an impossible task. I thought about lying on my back and letting the air in my waders float me down to more shallower water, but that would certainly have meant losing my fish. There was only one way to go and that was forward, but at least my toes were touching the bottom and the fish was still on. What a fool I must have been. Had I been giving advice to some young angler it would certainly have been a case of do as I say, not as I do. By luck, the Grim Reaper had been busy elsewhere that night and I was relieved when my feet finally landed flat on the river bed. I pushed towards the far side, the water thankfully getting shallower, until I was finally able to grab on to the tree roots and haul myself up the bank.

From here the battle could resume, but it would not be easy. Overhanging trees lined the bank, which meant that I would have to keep the rod low and close to the surface. The fish dashed from one side of the river to the other, then turned and rushed at speed towards me, making me take in line as fast as I could go. Then it shot downstream once again but close to the bank this time, which caused me much concern due to the tree roots that, even in the dark, I could see creeping like huge snakes down into the water. By having to keep the rod so low it was difficult to exert any real control. The fish made a powerful dash into the tree roots and then came that awful sad feeling of defeat as the line went slack. After all I had endured, risking my life even. Although I might have returned my monster, I would still have given anything just to have slipped the net under it, to have lifted it clear, to admire it if only for a moment or two.

I pulled off my chest waders and emptied them out. Then I stripped off and wrung my clothes out as best I could. Although it had been a warm night, I was beginning to shake with cold – the chill that a good soaking brings. Perhaps a hot drink would do me good. Fortunately, the coffee in my flask was still hot. I drank the bitter sweet nectar and a few minutes later the chill began to ebb.

I must have looked a pretty sight standing naked amongst the trees. I imagined what would happen if the keeper came by. He would surely have me arrested. What a bloody fool I had been. I then thought about how I was going to explain things to my wife – a giant fish pulled me in, or the bank gave way. Yes, she might go for that one – but I knew she wouldn't. She would know that I had been on yet another of my mad adventures. I quickly put my soaked clothes back on, hauled up my chest waders, which still had half an inch of water in the feet, and tried to gather myself together. I then made my way through the woods until I found a shallow place to wade back over and collect the spare rod I had left behind. I wasn't going to risk an ordeal like that one again.

It might be hard to believe but the story of that night's fishing doesn't end there. As I neared the ornamental bridge, the temptation to have a cast or two in that beautiful run below it became too much to bear. I was now convinced that a good fish must be lying there. I then began to question my own sanity. Surely if I had any brains at all I would get back and take a hot shower. Yes, that's what I'd do, but then again… That's when I heard a splashing noise under the bridge, a sound that made me think that otters must be playing. Any chance of a fish there would be ruined by now, but it would be nice to end such an eventful night by getting a glimpse of these fabulous animals. I slowed my pace and approached the bridge as quietly and with as much caution as possible, while trying to avoid stepping on a twig or brush too heavily against the trees. The splashing continued and I got an occasional glimpse of the disturbance of the water, but through the dense bushes, trees and other vegetation, I was still unable to make out the otters. I crept nearer. More splashing, and slowly I began to realise that it was not otters that were causing this disturbance. I strained to see what it was but still couldn't get a clear view. Perhaps a cow or a deer, but whatever it was, it was definitely not otters. It then occurred to me that it might be poachers netting the river. The splashing continued as I crept nearer still, but I still couldn't see through the trees. Curiosity got the better of me. I aimed my torch under the bridge and switched it on. There was a shriek and, caught like rabbits in the headlights of a car, a young couple were standing completely naked in the middle of the pool. They splattered and struggled to conceal their embarrassment behind a towel hardly bigger than a dishcloth. I don't know who was most surprised, me or them. To save them further embarrassment I switched the torch of. 'Oh, sorry,' I said.

'We're camping in the field over there,' called the young man who most likely thought I was a gamekeeper. 'Hope you don't mind. We were only bathing.' 'That's okay,' I replied. 'I've just been for a dip myself.' I made a fast and squelchy exit over the bridge.

The dressing

Hooks	Two size 8 long shank bucktail streamer hooks (tail and leading hook)
Silk	Optional
Body	(Tail hook) Holographic flat silver
Body	(Leading hook) Holographic flat silver (ending a little short of the eye)
Rib	None
Wing	(Tied in before the hackle) About ten peacock herl fibres with a few strands of black Minor Flash mixed in. The wing should end opposite the point of the tail hook
Hackle	Long 'teal' or pale-blue cock hackle fibres tied in alongside the wing (cheeks) and at the throat
Eyes	Two pearl beads about ¼in diameter. Due to the weight of the beads it is best to tie them in on the underside of the shank. This will prevent the lure from swimming upside down
Length	2½in

Construction

The mount is constructed in the same fashion as other similar lures (*see* Figure 24) using two size 8 long shank hooks.

The tinsel body is covered with Araldite super glue.

For the eyes, thread the two beads onto a length of 10–15lb BS nylon. They are then secured by tying them in tightly in criss-cross fashion behind the eye. The excess nylon is then snipped off and the whipping secured with the Araldite super glue, which will also give it a high gloss finish. Alternatively, for the eyes, you could use plastic Lumi beads. If you wish to add more

The pool under the bridge on the River Fowey below Bodmin Park Railway Station. This pool is much liked by salmon, sea trout and bathers!

A typical Waddington Shank lure. This one is dressed with a silver body and a wing of yellow and black goat hair fibres. The addition of eyes gives the lure a deadly appearance.

weight to the lure you could use Lumi metal beads, which are brass beads with a luminous powder coating. Both products are marketed by most leading suppliers.

WADDINGTON SHANKS

These were developed by Richard Waddington, the original intention being that the body could be dressed on the shank while a treble hook of appropriate size is fixed in the loop. However, few fly fishermen fix the hook in the loop these days. Most prefer to use a short piece of silicone tube, which is pushed onto the loop and the treble hook recessed into it. The only problem with this is that the tube distracts to some extent from the dressing itself, although the use of the tube to keep the hook straight is, in my opinion, a better idea because the hook will pull away from the shank when a fish takes and prevent the fish from levering itself free.

Waddington Shanks come in different sizes, but because they weigh heavier than a hook of comparable length they are very useful, particularly the larger sizes, for getting the lure to fish deep. For this reason I have included them under this chapter heading. I must stress here, however, that Waddington shanks are not high in my preference list. It would be better if it were possible to simply dress the fly on an extra long shank treble. Although some companies do advertise long shank treble hooks, I have so far been unable to find one that was long enough for my liking. How useful it would be to be able to have a sea trout treble long enough to eliminate the use of awkward Waddington shanks. However, some anglers think they are great and have much success on them. To be fair, some years ago Robert McHaffie sent me a few flies dressed on Waddington shanks, which I caught a lot of sea trout on. The best of these was called the Red Minnow, the dressing of which will follow shortly. Also, more recently, Karl Humphries sent me one of his own dressings on a Waddington, which is a version of a Silver Stoat Tail and one on which he has personally caught plenty of sea trout.

Like tube flies, the problem with Waddington shanks is keeping the hook held in line, thus preventing it from dangling away from the shank and swimming awkwardly. Also, a dangling treble is all the more likely to catch round the line when casting. While some dressers make use of a short piece of tubing to keep the hook in line, the method I give below when describing Robert McHaffie's pattern is not so bulky and takes nothing away from the dressing as a piece of tubing might. Instead it makes use of nylon to hold the treble hook in line.

RED MINNOW

The dressing

Hook	Size 8 Partridge X1BL treble hook
Shank	35mm Partridge double Waddington shank
Silk	Red
Body	First a short length of fluorescent red tape as a butt. This is followed by flat holographic silver tinsel to a halfway point along the shank where the first hackle is wound on. The upper half of the body is again the flat holographic tinsel
Rib	Fine round silver tinsel or wire
Hackles	A cock hackle dyed bright claret-red is wound on at a point half way along the shank

and a natural red game hackle is wound on at the throat

Head	Red

Note: If you are unable to obtain any fluorescent red tape you can varnish over the tying silk with fluorescent red varnish.

Construction

1. Fix the treble hook in the vice and wind on a bed of tying silk. Take a short length of nylon line about 8lb BS and thread one end through the eye in one direction and the other end through the eye from the opposite direction. Pull the two ends until the loop pulls firmly into the fork of the hook. Whip the nylon neatly to the shank and varnish over with black varnish (Figure 25A).

2. Once the varnish has dried, clip the treble to the Waddington shank and fix the upturned eye of the shank in the vice. The nylon strands that emerge from the treble should lie neatly on either side of the shank between the wire. This way a neat round body can be dressed (*see* Figure 25B). Tie down the nylon strands as you continue to wind on a bed of tying silk. Snip off the excess ends of the nylon below the eye. The treble and Waddington shank should now lie neatly in line.

3. At the eye end of the shank, catch in a length of the fine round silver ribbing. Cut a thin strip of the red fluorescent strip about $1/8$in wide and wind on a few turns as a butt. (The self-adhesive plastic used for display purposes is ideal.) Alternatively, varnish over the tying silk with fluorescent red varnish.

4. Above the butt, tie in a length of the holographic silver tinsel and wind this to a point about halfway along the

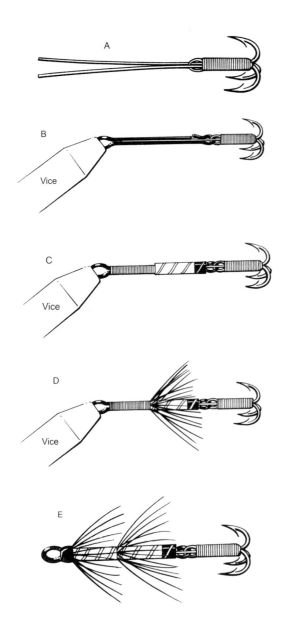

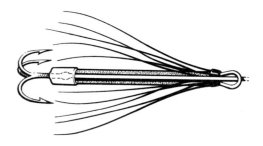

Figure 26. A simpler way to dress the Waddington shank and to attach the hook. The leader is passed through the leading eye, then alongside the shank, then through a short piece of tubing before it is tied to the treble hook. The tubing is then pushed onto the rear eye and the hook pulled into it.

Figure 25. Construction of the Red Minnow. See text for instructions.

three or four turns while stroking the fibres backwards at the same time. Tie the hackle down well and snip off the root (Figure 25D).

6   Catch in another length of the ribbing and the flat tinsel. Wind the tinsel to the eye and follow this up with the ribbing as in the lower section.

7   We now have to tie in the 'throat' hackle, which is a natural red cock hackle. Again, stroke the fibres backwards as you tie it in. Snip off the hackle root and continue with the silk to form the head, which can be varnished with red varnish. Complete the lure by painting on yellow eyes with red or black centres (Figure 25E).

This lure also has its uses in the early part of the night when dressed on smaller shanks, for instance on a 10mm shank with a size 16 treble hook.

A much simpler way to dress a Waddington shank is to forget about attaching the hook. All you have to do is place the shank in the vice and dress over it as when dressing a hook. Then pass the leader through the leading eye (the upturned one), down along the side of the body and out again through the rear eye. The leader is then

shank. Wind the wire or round tinsel over this as a ribbing and tie in (Figure 25C).

5   Tie in the first hackle, which is a cock hackle dyed bright claret-red. Wind on

passed through a short length of silicone tube, which fits tightly over the eye. The treble hook is then pulled into the tube (*see* Figure 26).

One more Waddington dressing is given below.

SILVER STOAT TAIL

This is based on one similar to that sent to me by Karl Humphries. It is good for getting down deep in the middle of the night. Again, it should be fished as slowly as possible. This is a much favoured lure on the River Towy where it has accounted for many double-figure sea trout, or sewin as they are called in Wales.

The dressing

Hook	Size 8 treble hook
Shank	35mm Partridge V1B
Silk	Black
Rib	Medium oval silver
Body	Holographic silver tinsel
Wing	Black stoat's tail or black squirrel tail. A few strands of black Mirror Flash are added in. This is not entirely black but is speckled with a variety of other colours
Head	Black

Anticipating a good take. The author fishing a good pool on a Lakeland stream.

14 Dry Flies

With the exception of dapping flies, which are used on lochs, conventional dry flies are rarely a part of the sea trout anglers armoury. This is mainly due to the fact that the majority of sea trout fishing is done in the dark and seeing them on the water would be almost impossible. If you asked sea trout fishermen what dry flies they used most, they would probably think you were joking, but the truth is that sea trout can, and often are, taken on a dry fly, and not always in the hours of daylight. Perhaps more sea trout than we realise are taken this way. I am sure that many a fly fisher out in pursuit of brown trout has taken a sea trout from time to time without ever realising the difference. Although he may have noticed that some of his fish were more silvery than others. In the dark, I have known a number of occasions when a sea trout has taken a wet fly off the surface before it has had time to sink. So it is not unreasonable to assume that dry flies have a part to play in the catching of sea trout. Moreover, there are times when a conventional dry fly will work when all others have failed. To illustrate the point I will relate to a time when Emelio Mutti and I went to fish on the River Ribble above Clitheroe.

It was a warm, overcast evening towards the end of July when we made our way across the meadow towards the river. Our path eventually took us for a short distance along the side of a little brook, which on previous occasions we had paid little regard to except for making the odd remark that it might hold a few good chub or possibly the odd brown trout. We had never seriously thought about fishing it due to the fact that all along its course towards the river it is overhung by dense bushes and brambles. As we passed the only place where it was possible to see through the vegetation we heard a loud splash. It sounded distinctively like the rising of a good fish, so, driven by curiosity, we climbed over the fence to take a closer look. There under the bushes we could make out the shadows of about six decent-sized fish, which we thought might possibly be sea trout. Because of the dark shadows and the failing light it was hard to say for certain. Armed with only fly tackle, fishing for them was an impossible task. The only way we could have fished this spot would have been with a worm, but even that would have been a difficult operation. We concluded that these fish were probably chub and continued down to the river where the brook enters.

The river was on its bones after weeks without rain but remarkably there were plenty of sea trout up. We were looking forward to some sport once the sun went down. For now though it was too early to start sea trout fishing. Emelio took himself down the river to a pool that he knew held a good head of brown trout. I, on the other hand, crossed the mouth of the brook, which was very shallow, and made my way up the river to fish a pool above those that I later intended to fish for sea trout. I thought this pool might offer some good brown trout fishing – which it did.

I fished my chosen pool until it was almost dark and took some nice brownies on a little sedge pattern that was similar to the natural kind that were hatching in abundance. Eventually it was dark enough to think about catching sea trout, which were already plopping here and there. I changed my fly to a small Medicine and made my way back down the river where I hoped I might meet up with Emelio and discuss tactics for the night. I found my friend fishing the pool where the brook enters and asked him if he had had any luck. With a broad smile he opened his bag to show me two fat sea trout weighing a little over 2lb apiece, which he told me he had taken on an Iron Blue Dun dressed in the Klinkhamer style. 'Look', he said, pointing towards the pool. I saw an amazing sight. Big sea trout were cruising about, creating bow waves like small torpedoes. Some were even swimming round with their backs out of the water. This was all the more surprising because this pool is a shallow one, not more than two feet or so at its deepest. Every now and again a fish would swim at speed into the ripple at the mouth of the brook, which was only a few inches deep. Some ran a short distance

and, as if deciding that it was too shallow, turned back. Some of the smaller fish were more determined. They wriggled their way through the shallows and continued at speed up the brook, making a bow wave as they went. The fish we had observed earlier in the brook must have been sea trout.

Emelio told me that he had tried casting in various places about the pool, but each time the fly had come into position under the bank downstream of the brook's mouth, he had hooked a fish. He invited me to try it for myself, so I put on a similar fly to Emelio's and started to fish. I tried at the head of the pool, the middle of the pool and even at the tail without an offer. Then I cast immediately under the bank where Emelio had suggested, and which was probably no more than six inches deep, and got an immediate take from a fish of similar weight to what Emelio had caught previously. He invited me to try again, so I cast about the pool without an offer and only when the fly was cast to the same place was any interest shown. Another fish of similar weight was soon hooked.

It is no secret that sea trout are attracted to the mouths of streams and to fish where

The mouth of a brook on the River Ribble. Sea trout are attracted to the mouths of brooks like this one and in low water can be seen cruising about in the vicinity.

123

one enters will often be rewarding. It is these small streams up which sea trout enter to spawn. Some are so small that you would never imagine that fish would, or could, get up them, but they do. Not long ago I was out with Chris Slater, who is the keeper on the Cumbrian Leven. As we drove down a back road towards Newby Bridge, Chris pulled into the side of the road where he pointed out a stream, if stream is the word, which was little more than a peat-stained trickle hardly more than a foot wide and three inches deep. It oozed through a wood before falling down the hillside to the river some forty feet below. He told me that a week earlier he had discovered a pair of sea trout spawning in that very place. How they had arrived here was beyond me but such is the determination of these amazing fish.

I am familiar with a place on the River Lune where a small stream enters and where, on another occasion, a dry fly did the trick. Again, this could hardly be described as a stream as it is no more than a drainage channel that runs along the side of some fortunate person's garden before it spills into the river towards the tail end of what is usually a productive salmon and sea trout pool. Over the seasons Emelio and I had noted that there was always a big sea trout in residence just below the mouth of this 'stream' and close to the bank where a giant of a willow tree droops. Every time we had fished here a big sea trout crashed in the same place, but casting over it from our bank is extremely difficult as the river is wide here and too deep to wade. It is only just possible to reach the spot by long hauling a weight forward line and even then the willow tree only adds to the problem. But it never prevented us from trying. There was hardly a time when we fished here that we didn't try for that elusive big fish. We tried all the usual lures, including wake lures, without success until we grew tired of trying and wandered off to fish easier places.

On a dark night in early September we were walking down the river. As we neared the same place, as if on cue, a big sea trout crashed in exactly the same place as before. We both looked at each other, shrugged, and continued on. That fish would never be caught, not unless the owner of the house opposite gave us permission to fish from his lawn which, from what we had heard, was highly unlikely. He was known locally as the village grump.

As we walked further down the river the big fish crashed once again. The temptation to have yet another try for it was too much. I just had to go for it, so I took off the double tapered line and replaced it with a weight forward. Now to choose the right fly. It occurred to me that the only thing that had never been tried before was a dry fly, so I put on a Daddy Longlegs for no particular reason other than this was the time of year when the natural variety was about. After a few false casts the line was shot across the wide river and landed with a flop, which I hoped would not disturb my fish. I knew that I had placed the fly exactly where I wanted it and that it would soon drift under the willow by the mouth of the stream. I held my breath.

The fish crashed again, but this time it had taken my offering. It bolted upstream towards the bridge before turning and taking a high speed tour of the big pool. It was certainly a big fish, perhaps approaching double figures. Next it ran past me towards the tail of the pool before turning and heading back towards the bridge. I must have had it on for almost ten minutes before I finally got ready with the net. But just as I was about to slip the net under it the fly parted company with the fish and shot through the air. The big fish was lost, but as a poor consolation prize I did catch the barbed wire fence behind me.

In both the above-mentioned cases the dry fly worked close to the mouth of a stream and within a very short distance downstream of it. Why this should be is something I can't explain. I could understand it if the fish were stationed in the mouth of the stream in much the same way as a brown trout might when waiting for food to come drifting by. But in each case the 'taking' fish were under the bank and out of the flow of the incoming stream. Is it perhaps that they have a greater sense of security in this position and are, therefore, more likely to take? All of this is, of course, only speculation and I don't think that I will ever know the real answer. I can only tell you that I have fished the dry fly in similar circumstances with reasonable success. All this was in the dark, so let's turn to fishing a dry fly in the day.

The first sea trout I took on a dry fly was from the River Annan. It was a fine, warm afternoon and to kill some time before the evening (when I anticipated fishing seriously) I took a walk along the bank with the trout rod, in search of wild brown trout or chub. Eventually I arrived at a quiet bend where the stream ran smoothly beneath overhanging willows on the far bank. One or two fish were rising to a hatch of olives, a dimple of a rise that suggested chub rather

than trout. I put on a hackled Gold Ribbed Hare's Ear and flicked it neatly upstream of the willows. Down it came, perfectly on course until it was over the rising fish. A dimple. The rod was raised and my first thought was that I was into a hefty chub. Chub? – it was definitely no chub! The fish suddenly shot down the pool with me in pursuit and after a lengthy tussle I had it in the net – a fine sea trout of 2½lb. I returned to my original site and again put out the GRH. Down it came again, nicely under the willows, and again a dimple. I struck and another sea trout went charging down the pool. But this one, which was a little larger, was more athletic than his mate. He leaped high out of the water and was gone. I fished all afternoon in the hope that a third one would rise to the dry fly, but to no avail.

On another occasion I was fishing the River Liddle, again on a warm, sunny afternoon. My intention was no more than to pass away the time by having a little fun with the small native brown trout, which had been rising freely for the past hour or more on the quiet, streamy pool. But the tranquillity was disturbed by a herd of heifers arriving to drink, just a little upstream

A nice ripple under the trees and a good place to fish a dry fly.

125

on the opposite bank. The activity of the beasts soon turned the water muddy brown and, cursing the inoffensive creatures, I decided to move upstream to an undisturbed pool. But I noticed that fish were still rising, albeit in the coloured water. Were the heifers churning up nymphs or other particles of food? I cast again and the fly was seized immediately by a much bigger and stronger fish. It turned out to be a 3lb sea trout, not a fresh fish. I cast again and once more the fly was taken with gusto by another 3lb sea trout. Two more were lost before the cattle moved on and the water began to clear. All I could catch after that were more small brownies. Exactly why the sea trout had come on the feed whilst the water had been coloured I am unsure, but it had been a nice bonus to the afternoon.

Over the years, the subject of catching sea trout on a dry fly has been raised on countless occasions with anglers around the UK and from abroad, and from these many conversations the following generalisations have been reached. However, I should point out that this summary is a distillation of the experiences of many anglers. It is not based on the findings of any scientific survey.

1   The majority were taken on sunnier days between 11am and 4pm.
2   The best months were June and July.
3   The river was at summer level.
4   A wide variety of flies were given, but the six that were mentioned most were Black Gnat, Coch-y Bondhu, Greenwell's Glory, Hare's Ear, Iron Blue Dun and March Brown.

It is interesting to note that when asked if they had been attempting to match a hatch of flies that was on the water at the time, most said that they hadn't.

The above account of dry flies was described back in 1985 and, although it has mainly been with brown trout in mind, I have carried the same dressings in my box ever since as they represent a wide enough variety to enable me to match most naturals that might be on the water at any given time. Over the years fashions have changed and I have come to believe that dry flies dressed Klinkhamer style, after its inventor Hans van Klinken, are more successful. The majority of my dry flies are now dressed this way. It is a great parachute fly that rides low in the water and is easier to see, especially when dressed using white antron wool for the wing post, which makes the fly bi-visible. But what of sea trout?

In 1998 Emelio Mutti and I agreed to carry out an experiment by fishing through the night using only dry flies consisting of the above-named patterns dressed Klinkhamer style on size 12 hooks. This experiment was undertaken on the River Lune on a warm and overcast night in August when the river was low, yet holding a good head of sea trout. The area we chose to fish is called the 'Flats'. It is a long, flat, calm stretch of water with hardly any movement except for a very slow run under the opposite bank, which is overhung with occasional willow trees. We had previously caught brown trout along this stretch in the evening using a wide range of dry flies. We had also caught the occasional sea trout in the night on wet flies and lures, but we had never caught sea trout on dry flies here.

Sea trout were beginning to show along the Flats, and starting at about 10pm when there was still a hint of light left, Emelio was the first to catch a fish on his chosen Greenwell's Glory – a reasonable brown trout. Shortly after I caught a similar brown trout. Emelio caught four more brown trout and I caught one more before midnight, but still no sea trout. We took a short break in which Emelio changed to a Gold Ribbed Hare's Ear and I changed to a Coch-y-Bondhu. Neither of us took another fish until about 1am when I got a take from something bigger. After a good fight the first sea trout, weighing 2lb, was landed. Around 1.30am Emelio took another brown trout. A few minutes later he caught his first sea trout, which also weighed 2lb. Although no fish were now showing to give us any encouragement, we continued to fish with dry flies, although we both knew that fishing a sunk lure would be more productive. Around 2am there was a clatter on the surface and my friend was doing battle with a sea trout that weighed 3¾lb. Nothing happened after that until about 3am when we both hooked into a fish at almost the same time. I had changed to a March Brown while Emelio had changed back to a Greenwell's Glory. Both fish weighed 2lb. By the first glimmer of dawn only one other fish had been taken, which was another brown trout that Emelio took on the same Greenwell's. But I had work to do that day and it was time for me to leave. Emelio fished on into the dawn light and took another sea trout of 3lb at around 5am. This exercise proved little but we did have fun and I was left with no doubt that sea trout are there for the catching on a dry fly, with a bit of perseverance, of course.

Here are the dressings for the six favourite Klinkhamer parachute dry flies. The novice might encounter difficulty, so I have given tying instructions for the first one. But first:

1 It is important that you can see the fly on the water, especially in poor light. For this reason the wing post (which is actually the wing) should not be snipped too short.
2 Use only the best premium hackles as the fly is supported only by the fibres of the parachute.
3 When winding the hackle on you should wind from the top down.
4 Use floatant only on the wing, not on the body.

BLACK GNAT

Hooks	Size 16–10 Partridge 15 BN Klinkhamer, or Kamasan B420 sedge hooks
Silk	Black
Rib	Fine silver wire
Body	Black seal fur (or substitute)
Wing post	White antron wool
Thorax	Peacock herl
Hackle	Black cock hackle
Head	Black

Construction

For this purpose we will use a size 10 hook, which is a good size to practise with.

1 Fix the hook firmly in the vice and wind on a bed of the silk in touching turns from the eye to halfway round the bend. Now catch in the ribbing (Figure 27A).
2 Wax the silk with liquid wax and dub on a thin rope of the seal fur. Wind this (the body) up to within ⅛in of the eye and remove any excess seal fur.
3 Wind on the ribbing to end in the same position as the body, i.e. ⅛in short of the eye. *Do not trim off* at this stage (Figure 27B).
4 Tie in a single piece of antron wool across the back of the hook (Figure 27C).
5 Pull the two ends of the antron wool, along with the ribbing, upwards. This will form the wing post. Wind the silk tightly around the base of the post and around the shank to make the wool stand (Figure 27D).
6 Behind the wing post catch the hackle stem and two or three strands of peacock herl (Figure 27E).
7 Make two turns of the herl behind the wing post and two turns above it

127

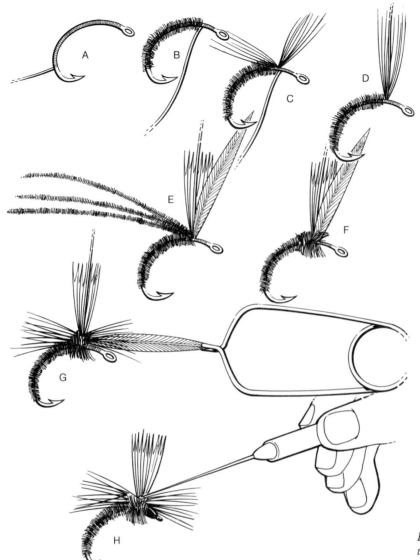

Figure 27. Construction of the Black Gnat. See text for instructions.

to form the thorax. Tie in and snip off the excess (Figure 27F).

8   Carefully wind on the hackle around the base of the wing post (four or five turns should be enough, winding from the top down), so that the hackle lies horizontally around the post, forming a parachute wing (Figure 27G).

9   Take hold of the ribbing and *carefully* pull it down between the wound hackle. Then take a couple of turns behind the eye. Tie this in very tightly. This is *important* as it will stop the hackle from slipping up the wing post. Continue with the silk to form a small head.

A Black Gnat dry fly dressed in the Klinkhamer parachute style.

10 You can now carefully apply a touch of clear varnish to the head and on the hackle where it is wound around the wing post. It is best to use your dubbing needle to do this. Put a drop on the point and apply it (Figure 27H). Snip the wing post to the required length.

GOLD RIBBED HARE'S EAR

Hooks	Size 16–10 Partridge 15 BN Klinkhamer, or Kamasan B420 sedge hooks
Silk	Brown
Rib	Fine gold wire
Body	Hare body fur or hare mask
Wing post	White antron wool
Thorax	Peacock herl
Hackle	Light natural red/brown cock hackle
Head	Brown. The silk varnished over

IRON BLUE DUN

Hooks	Size 16–10 Partridge 15 BN Klinkhamer, or Kamasan B420 sedge hooks
Silk	Grey
Rib	Fine silver wire
Tag	Magenta floss
Body	Lightly dubbed mole fur
Wing post	White antron wool
Thorax	Peacock herl
Hackle	Darkish grey/blue dun cock hackle
Head	Grey. The silk varnished over

GREENWELL'S GLORY

Hooks	Size 16–10 Partridge 15 BN Klinkhamer, or Kamasan B420 sedge hooks
Silk	Pale primrose waxed with cobbler's wax
Rib	Fine gold wire
Body	The waxed tying silk
Wing post	White antron wool
Thorax	Peacock herl
Hackle	Greenwell/Furnace cock hackle
Head	The silk varnished

MARCH BROWN

Hooks	Size 16–10 Partridge 15 BN Klinkhamer, or Kamasan B420 sedge hooks
Silk	Brown
Rib	Yellow tying silk
Body	Hare fur and brown seal fur (or substitute) mixed together

Wing post	White antron wool		*Silk*	Brown
Thorax	Peacock herl		*Rib*	Red single Glo Brite floss
Hackle	(Two hackles) Red brown cock hackle and speckled partridge hackle		*Body*	Bronze peacock herl
			Wing post	White antron wool
Head	The silk varnished		*Thorax*	Peacock herl
			Hackle	Red brown cock hackle
			Head	The silk varnished

COCH-Y-BONDHU

Hooks	Size 16–10 Partridge 15 BN Klinkhamer, or Kamasan B420 sedge hooks

Emelio Mutti fishing the 'Flats' on the River Lune. This is a long and calm stretch of river and much care is required not to disturb the water when wading at night. It was here that we fished all night using only dry flies and where we both caught sea trout.

15 Pot Holes and Other Awkward Places

I doubt if there is a sea trout river anywhere in the UK that, at least for part of its course, does not tumble and force its way through dark, deep gorges and giant rock formations. This is where only the brave or the brainless go to fish the pot-like deep pools with a worm for salmon and sea trout when the river is up and coloured. I can think of many places that fit this description. The River Ogwen and parts of the upper River Dovey, where I sometimes fish, are like this. So too is much of the River Lune above Sedbergh and on towards Tebay. There are places here where the angler needs to be something of a mountain goat to fish, but such is the urge that quite often the dangers of fishing these places are usually ignored. But the Lune is a river that pulls me like a magnet, as it did on this particular August morning.

I had arrived on the water very early to find that it was still a few inches above normal summer level and, as chance would have it, still a little stained from the downpour of rain the previous day. There was still a chance of a salmon so I hastily tackled up my worming rod with a bunch of lobs on the end. The hardest part was getting down to the water's edge through the great boulders, but at length I was in my favourite spot where I had caught a salmon or two in the past. The usual lie is under a huge flat rock that overhangs a deep cauldron of a hole. But to see if anything was lying under it meant crawling on my belly and peering over the edge, a dangerous and difficult thing to do. Even with polarised glasses on it took a

little time for my eyes to focus through the stained water, but there it was, just where I'd expected it to be, a salmon that looked to be at least 15lb. I slithered back over the rock and manoeuvred myself into a position a few yards upstream of the fish. I then cast in a little upstream and allowed the current to bring the offering down to touch bottom just above where the salmon was lying. The fish wasted no time at all in taking the bait.

A difficult place to fish the fly.

131

First a tug. I waited a few seconds. Tug. I gave it a little slack line. Tug, tug, and then a harder pull. I lifted the rod and the fish was on. What a fight it put up in that heavy fast water. First it ran down the river into the next deep hole below, with me scrambling over the slippery rocks to keep a tight line on it. Then it decided to turn and head back upstream to where the fight had begun. I scrambled back over the rocks and at one stage lost my footing and fell heavily on my backside, almost sliding over the edge of the flat overhang. But I somehow managed to get to my feet and down to the water's edge where I continued the battle until the fish finally came to the net. It was indeed a fish to remember, a lovely fresh fish that must have run hard from the sea, which was at least 25 miles away.

For the rest of the morning I tried hard to catch a second salmon but had no further luck. I had located another salmon and had passed the bunch of worms by it until my arm was aching. I had even tapped it on the nose on more than one occasion, but the fish remained completely oblivious to the offering. By midday the river had dropped considerably and was now running quite clear, no longer the best of conditions for worming. So I decided to head down to a lower and easier part of the river and fish the dry fly for brow trout.

Reluctantly I threw what remained of my bag of worms into the river – might as well give the brownies a treat – and started to climb back up the steep rocks to safer ground. Looking back down the river I happened to see something flash in a pot a little way down from where I had fished earlier. I wondered at first if I had imagined it; sea trout often flash like this as they flip on their sides. The temptation to investigate was just too compelling, so I climbed back down for a better look. There in a hole, rather than a pool, some 10ft deep by about 15ft wide, was a sight to set the nerves tin-

gling – a shoal of at least 100 sea trout that ranged from 2lb to one that I guessed was easily 6lb. How I regretted throwing those worms away; clear or not I would certainly have dropped a worm amongst this lot. But now the water was quite clear I would have more chance with a small fly. But fly fishing a pot hole like this, with fast water pushing the current hard, would be difficult.

I remembered a method that I had occasionally put to good use when reservoir fishing. I had often thought about trying it on a river but had never got round to it, dismissing it as a daft idea. On a reservoir it had worked when I had fished a Booby. This is a floating lure that is fished on a short leader at the end of a fast-sinking line. The Booby then floats just off the bottom. Perhaps now was the time to put the theory to the test. I returned to my car and put up my fly rod with a high density no. 8 line. Directly to the end of this I tied just two feet of 6lb BS leader. This was a little too fine perhaps for sea trout, but with the river now fairly low and clear and the sky getting bluer by the minute even this seemed too heavy. I thought about tying on a Booby but changed my mind in the full knowledge that no sea trout was ever that daft – not by day at least. But which fly? The only thing I could see that might work was a small Muddler Minnow, a type of floating lure made from deer hair. It did not float as good as a Booby but it was worth a try, especially if I gave it a good soaking in Permafloat.

Now I was back over that pot full of fish and wondering if, in fact, the line would get down in the fast water that gushed across the surface. I cast to the tail end of the pool, or rather across the hole. My intention was to get the fly to sink to the bottom at a point behind the shoal rather than risk it sinking amongst the fish and causing them to panic, but the current was far too strong and held the line near the surface. This was never going to work. If I had had any shot I would have attached one or two to the end of the fly line. One way or another I just had to get the line to sink, so in desperation I slowly pushed the end of the rod down into the water. This worked and I watched the line begin to sink slowly until at last it lay along the bottom just to the side of the shoal that, fortunately, had not seemed concerned. Next, I slowly retrieved until I could clearly see the Muddler right in the middle of the shoal, but they showed no interest as it passed between them. It was time to lift out and begin the procedure over again. Then, just as I lifted the rod, I saw a fish make a sudden dash at the fly. In my excitement – an instinctive response – I struck so hard that the fly shot through the air and caught itself in a dead tree root. So much for experience. Idiot! Start again.

It had occurred to me that the fly had been attacked as it had accelerated, so this time I worked the fly in short but steady pulls as it passed through the shoal. The big one hit the Muddler so hard that the rod

was almost wrenched from my grip. Round and round the pot it tore before attempting to bore into every corner and crevice. How I wished that I had used a heavier leader, but it was too late for that now. I would have to play this fish with every ounce of patience and skill. The fight seemed to go on forever before my fish finally came to the surface. Getting the net under it, however, was going to be extremely difficult. As I inched the fish nearer and nearer I was aware that at any second it might find a new lease of life or the force of the current at the surface would put too much strain on the leader. I lay on my stomach and reached out as far as I dared over the slippery rock, praying that I wouldn't go sliding over to join the fish in the deep hole. While still attempting to keep the rod high in my right hand and straining to reach out with my left, I strained my back and a searing pain shot between my shoulder blades. If I had stretched another inch I might well have gone for a swim, but by some miracle the fish obliged by swimming straight into the net.

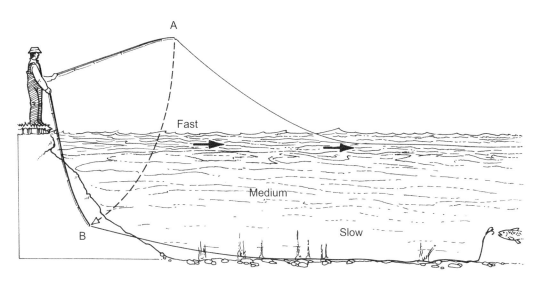

Figure 28. (A) The line is held in the fast water at the surface. (B) When the rod is pushed under the surface the line sinks. The floating fly is attached to a short leader and floats up just above the river bed in the 'Booby' fashion.

I inched myself back over the rock until I felt safe enough to get to my feet. I cursed the pain in my back, then looked at the fabulous fish in the net. It was truly a case of the agony and the ecstasy.

Jigging

When I was in my late teens I would often go worming on a small stream that flows into Loch Long. To me, this stream, which tumbles steeply down the mountainside through great boulders and chasms, was a magical place of dramatic beauty where I could usually fish all day and never see another soul. Summer was a great time to catch the small brown trout that haunt the rocky pools. They were not big – a four-ounce fish was considered a good one – but they were good fun to catch. By August, providing we had a spate, sea trout would be tempted to run up from the loch and occasionally I caught some nice ones. Considering the size of the stream, this was quite remarkable.

One night in early September there was a storm and the rain lashed down all night. I didn't sleep well that night. It wasn't the sound of the storm that prevented me

Here I am jigging for a sea trout lying under the bank on the River Nith. Patience and nerves of steel are often called for when attempting this.

from sleeping, it was the thought of those sea trout that must surely be running my stream. By 6am the storm was beginning to subside. I dressed in a hurry, grabbed a round of toast and a swig of milk and was off.

It was still raining as I made my way up the muddy sheep track, but here and there the sun was attempting to break through the black clouds with the promise of better weather to follow, and a sea trout or two. What could be better than a pool full of fat fish all to myself. Perhaps not. I looked down to see footprints in the mud. Someone had beaten me to it. I climbed to the top of a crag and looked down on the stream – my hot spot, my secret pool. Someone was fishing there. What cheek! I would have to fish the next pool down. This was a much harder pool to fish, although it was known to be a good holding pool. The man was slightly built and probably in his eighties, which made me wonder how he had managed to get up the steep track. But he had a kind face and seemed pleased to see me. 'Any luck?' I asked. He opened his bag to reveal three lovely sea trout of about 2lb each. 'No bad, eh?' No, not bad.

I scrambled down to the next pool, eager to get started, but when I opened my bag I realised that in my rush to get fishing I had forgotten to collect my tin of worms from under the shed. It would take me at least an hour to return for the worms, and that was if I ran. But the thought of losing so much fishing time when the stream was yielding fish was distressing. Feeling more than a little foolish, I approached the old man and asked him if he had any worms to spare. Seeing my predicament, he chuckled and pointed to a bulging cloth bag. 'Help yourself, son.'

I was soon fishing on the lower pool. It was more of a deep tub with a large rock jutting out over one side, which at least offered a wet seat. In the middle of the 'tub' I could see about ten silver sea trout. Trembling with anticipation I cast upstream and allowed my bunch of worms to trundle down to them. A two pounder took straight away and what a beautiful fresh fish it was. A little later I took another fish of about 2¾lb, which was followed by another one a little smaller. Through the corner of my eye I caught sight of the old man who was standing to my left. He pointed, 'There's a big yin under that stane'. I went to stand next to him and sure enough I could make out the shape of a much bigger fish lying close in under the very rock I had been sitting on.

While the old man sat and watched I tried from every angle available to get the bait under the rock and close to that fish, but it was impossible.

'Do ye want me tae show ye?' he asked.

'Sure' I replied, handing him my rod.

He removed the swivel and ledger weight and attached the hook directly to the end of the line. Immediately above the hook he squeezed on a large lead shot before selecting a single small worm, which he hooked on at its very end. Next, he lowered the worm down over the rock and began to jig it up and down. He explained that instead of trying to get the worm under the rock it would be easier to tempt the fish out from its lair. From my position I could see the worm wriggling in a tantalising manner as he slowly lifted it from the bottom then allowed it to sink quickly, then up again. This continued for about five minutes until I saw the big fish glide casually out from under the rock and take the worm, not by force, but a gentle take as if in slow motion. The old man lifted the rod and the fish was hooked. He indicated that I should take the rod, but it was his fish, he had caught it. I refused, but he insisted and almost pushed the rod into my hand. 'Go on, it's your fish son.' I reluctantly took the rod and

played the fish, which fought with powerful authority to the last. What a fish it was – 5lb of shimmering silver. 'No bad, eh?' said the old man. No, not bad.

What has this got to do with fly fishing you might ask. I'll tell you. Some years later I found myself in similar circumstances when fishing on a river in Wales. This time I detected a good sea trout that was not lying under an overhanging rock but under the shadow of a steep bank. I remembered the old man and the trick he had taught me. But I had no worms, only flies, none of which looked remotely like a worm. What I did have, however, was an elastic band that was holding the lid of my lunch box on. I cut the elastic band and hooked one end of it to my fly, which I think might have been a small Zulu. Above the hook I squeezed on a swan shot that had been rolling around in my jacket pocket for years. The offering was then duly lowered in front of the fish and jigged up and down. It appeared to be wriggling quite well, but would it work? Incredibly, it did. The fish took the elastic band fly with vigour and tore off down the river to begin a good fight. The fish was later returned, but it probably weighed about 2¾lb.

On the following day I again made my way to the same spot and was pleased to see that four or five sea trout were lying in the same place. The elastic band fly was lowered down and the jigging began. After a minute or two a fish took and bolted across the river. But almost as quick, I felt a twang and the fish came off. I reeled in to find only about half an inch of elastic left on the hook. A bungee-jumping fish perhaps? If it had not been Sunday I might have gone down to the local village shop and purchased a packet of elastic bands, but I knew they would be closed so I would have to think of something else, something which would wriggle. I couldn't use a worm as this was a fly-only water and I wasn't sure if an elastic band was legitimate. I would have to think of something else.

I took another look in my fly box but the only thing I could see that might wriggle a bit was a lead-headed Dog Nobbler type of lure, which I had found some years earlier stuck in a tree. But beggars can't be choosers, so I put it on and lowered it down under the bank. After a few minutes of jigging another fish took. It immediately exploded into action, tearing line from the reel and leaping. But this time the fish was well hooked and eventually it came to the net.

Those of you who have read my previous book *Sea Trout Flies* might recall my description of the Irt Jigger Nymph and how I lost a bet, a pint of John Peel to be precise. It had been a hot day and the River Irt, one of my favourite Cumbrian streams, was low and clear; not the best of conditions for catching sea trout by day. An old guy, who I had met once or twice and who knew the river well, pointed out to me a good fish of about 6lb that was lying under an overhanging shrub. I told him that it would be a waste of time trying for it in such conditions and in broad daylight too. But he bet me a pint that within an hour he would have it on the bank, and by legal means at that. The bet was readily accepted. The old man had no chance of tempting that fish, so I took up a position by the bridge from where I could watch the 'master' at work while dreaming about that pub in Ravenglass and the cool pint with frothy foam sliding slowly down the glass.

Just above where the fish lay was a small gap in the bushes through which the old man poked his rod. Keeping well concealed in the long grass he delicately flicked out a short line. Once the current had carried the fly towards where the fish lay he began to work the fly with a gentle raising and lowering of the rod. In a bygone age this method was known as dibbling. It is, in effect, a gentle form of jigging.

My daydream was broken when the old man, in a matter-of-fact tone, called 'He's on'. His rod was bent double as he fought

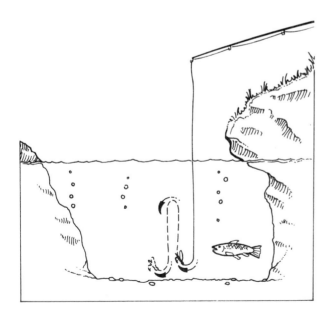

Figure 29. The jigging action of a fly weighted at the head. This is the method used to tempt a fish from under an overhanging rock or bank.

the fish which was well fired up. But as the fight came to a close I waded down under the bushes and netted it for him. The ale was as good as I had dreamed it would be – but it was on me.

The old man, whose name I am unable to remember (possibly because the beer was so good), later gave me one of his jigging lures, or rather nymphs, on which I have since caught a number of sea trout by copying his style.

The dressing

Hook	A size 10 4X long shank Partridge bucktail/streamer
Silk	Black
Tail	A few teal fibres tied in short
Body	Black seal's fur (or substitute) over the lower half and medium olive seal's fur over the upper half
Hackle	Two or three turns of natural red cock hackle behind the lead head
Rib	A few turns of fine round gold tinsel
Head	A size BB lead substitute shot painted black

137

16 Tidal Waters

ESTUARIES AND TIDAL POOLS

The estuaries I write of here are the estuaries as we might imagine them; places where dunlin, tents and oyster catchers feed at low tide, where seaweed clings to the shore and where the water is brackish as fresh mixes with salt in the final part of the river's journey to the sea. I do not mean the huge and deep estuaries, such as the River Mersey or the Humber, which are better described as shipping channels. I refer to the estuaries usually associated with game fishing rivers.

At low water many estuaries reveal pools and runs that are not too dissimilar from those found in the higher reaches of the river. These tidal pools can offer some excellent sea trout fishing. Fish, which failed to run up at the head of the incoming tide, will hold in these pools to feed while awaiting the next tide. You will often be amazed at how many sea trout are to be caught in them.

Although subject to the elevation of any particular river, above the actual estuary are usually found the pools and stretches where marine vegetation yields to reeds, rushes and other familiar plants and grasses. These are not tidal pools as such but pools that are forced to 'back up' by the incoming tide, to rise in level and to fall again as the tide ebbs. Put another way, the rising tide acts as a dam against the fresh water flowing down the river. Fishing tidal waters can

The author fishing the mouth of a small stream where it flows into the sea at the head of Loch Eil. It is here that some good sea trout have been taken after dark.

sometimes be difficult, if not dangerous at times, and a good knowledge of the tide, its height and times, is essential, as too are the best places to catch sea trout. As they say, you can't beat local knowledge.

Some estuaries are famous sea trout fisheries, such as the River Ythan in Aberdeenshire for instance. Although only a short river, it has a large estuary for the lower five miles of its course. This is just one of many that I could mention. There are countless estuaries that are not recognised in any way as sea trout fisheries, not because they are unproductive but simply because they are rarely fished. Quite often the angler is put off by the relatively short time available between stages of the tide, or there is too much weed, or the shoreline is muddy or too rocky. Some estuaries have a dangerous tide race, such as that of the River Kent in Cumbria where a klaxon is sounded as the tide is about to come in. It is only suitable for worm fishing from the relative safety of the higher shore. For the most part, however, the majority of estuaries and higher tidal-affected reaches are not so difficult to fish once you know how to go about it. Let's look at some typical examples.

The River Leven in Cumbria, for example, flows out of Lake Windermere and runs for little more than six miles before entering Morecambe Bay. For the first four miles of its journey seaward it flows through Newby Bridge then descends steeply, tumbling over waterfalls and weirs and through some of the most exciting and 'fishy' pools you ever did see. The river then continues by Haverthwaite (famous for its steam railway station and where you will find the appropriately named Anglers Arms) until it reaches Low Wood bridge. Just above the bridge is the start of a fabulous fast, streamy run, which continues under the bridge, then on for about 300 yards before finally petering out. From now onwards the river is sluggish and affected by the tide. On smaller tides the difference is hardly noticeable but bigger spring tides will push the river back to flood the first two pools above Low Wood bridge. Following the river's course, we pass the fishing hut and continue towards the disused railway bridge. From here the river starts to look more like an estuary as it gradually starts to widen. The grasses merge into salt marsh, providing an excellent habitat for nesting lapwings, curlews, and many other birds. It then reaches Greenod, where it becomes wide and enters Morecambe Bay. At first glance, the angler could be forgiven for thinking that this featureless lower section of river is not worth fishing, but bearing in mind that any migratory fish caught in the upper reaches of a river must first pass through the estuary to get there, then there is always a chance to catch them here. In fact, the catch returns from the lower section of the Leven are often greater than those of the upper reaches.

If there is enough rain and plenty of water flowing out of Lake Windermere, sea trout will enter the Leven as early as June but the main run usually starts in August. In very dry weather, when little fresh water is coming down, the sea trout will come in on the tide and linger on the lower section. Some will drop back to the sea while others will hold here and become 'resident' as they wait for rain. Other fish, and this is always the case with sea trout, will push on up the river regardless of the low water conditions. I am reminded of the 2005 season on the River Ribble. There was no rain for weeks on end, yet the river was literally stuffed with sea trout. In spite of the green algae caused by the dry weather, I seemed to hook on every other cast. I often drive folks round the bend by moaning about too much fine weather, but the fact is that without rain salmon and the bigger sea trout would be scarce, at least on the higher reaches of many rivers. In addition, a river needs a good flushing out from time to time to get rid of the accumulative algae and silt. The Leven is no exception – the more water that comes down the river, the more fish wafting out in Morecambe Bay will be encouraged to come in. Should the river be in spate, migratory fish will soon be distributed throughout the river system.

Providing there is enough pull on the current to work it, the Snake Fly, or similar lure, will almost certainly be successful in an estuary as sea trout fresh from the sea are usually taken easily on one. In a dry season, when there is hardly any fresh water coming down the river, the lower Leven becomes sluggish and dour and often difficult to fish. In my own experience, the best chance is at night using a surface lure.

Fortunately, in August and September we can expect a few spring tides and I would hate not to be on the river bank at such times. Even when there is hardly any fresh water coming down the river, sea trout, and salmon too, will still pour in on these big tides. But they will not be easy to catch while the tide is pushing up and the fish are running with it. However, once the tide turns and is flowing back to sea the

fish will be fooled for an hour or two into believing that the river is in spate and take with some relish. During this time I usually start with a 3in Snake Fly on a sinking line. As the level continues to fall I change to a shorter one of say 2½in and then to 2in as the river approaches its normal level. This advice applies to almost any river.

I once fished the lower tidal part of the Leven in the middle of a July heatwave. I don't know why I went so early in the day. I certainly didn't expect to catch much before dark but perhaps a willing fish or two had come in on the tide, although it was only a neap tide and hardly enough to make a difference. It was more likely that I just wanted to escape from writing and shake off the crick in my neck. As I had expected, the level was low with hardly any movement, but there were enough occasional sea trout jumping to keep me interested, although I didn't give much for my chances of catching one in the day. However, it was a beautiful day to be on the river and better than working. My son Chris, who prefers sea fishing, had been fishing for flatties down at Greenod, but after three hours without a bite he had decided to walk up the river

A sweeping bend on the estuary of the River Erne, Ballyshannon. Good sea trout fishing can be had along this shore.

to keep me company. After his long walk in the heat of the day, made more enduring by the weight of his tackle, he decided, after devouring the rest of my sandwiches, to take a nap on the river bank while I continued to flog away with the fly in what I had now considered to be little more than casting practice. Perhaps Chris had more sense than me, but I hate to be defeated.

As I wandered along the bank casting here and there I noticed some movement in the shallows near my feet. When I bent down for closer inspection I could see that the bottom was covered in tiny baby flounders not more than one inch long, which were skittering about in short jerky movements.

As I watched in fascination I couldn't believe what happened next. As one of the tiny flounders swam out of the shallows into slightly deeper water there was a sudden flash of silver as a large sea trout of about 5lb shot in and grabbed it. It had happened so fast that I was left wondering if I had dreamt it. I have seen sea trout attack whitebait and sand eels along the coast but I had never seen anything like this before. Then I remembered an old friend telling me that he had once gutted a sea trout that had contained a small flattie in its stomach.

My regular fishing buddy Emelio had recently returned from a trip to the Bahamas, where he had been fishing for bone fish. He had given me a couple of flies that he had tied for the occasion. These were based on a dressing he got from an American magazine and, although they were dressed to represent small crabs, to my mind they looked more like small flatties. (It might be worth mentioning here that I once caught a sea trout off the shore when fishing near Belmullet in County Mayo. A lovely fish of 1½lb which, when cleaned, contained the remains of three small crabs.) I couldn't remember if these lures were still

in the car but it might be worth the walk back through the wood to find out. Fortunately they were there and I soon returned and put one on with a sinking line.

I made my way upstream above Chris (who was now enjoying a good kip) to where the river takes a wide bend and is some 15 feet deep under the bank. I cast as far as I could across the river, waited for the line to sink and started to retrieve. I was hoping that a sea trout, perhaps the same one, would grab it but none did. I persevered in the sweltering heat while Chris snored on and the odd sea trout jumped out to laugh at me.

It eventually dawned on me that I might do better if I tried to imitate the short jerking movements of the tiny flounder. Give it another ten minutes and I would suggest going for a walk followed by a meal in the Anglers Arms. At dusk I would be back on the river armed with a surface lure. I cast again, but this time I retrieved in short, fast pulls. This made the lure hop across the bottom, a method known as 'strip strike'. Here's the technique.

Assuming that you are right handed, point the rod towards the lure then retrieve in short, fast pulls about one foot at a time. A slight tension on the line should be maintained between the rod handle and the first two fingers of the right hand, over which the line is drawn. Do not apply too much tension or a sudden take will almost certainly result in the leader being snapped. Once you feel a fish take, do not strike by lifting the rod but continue to strip, making a longer pull until your left hand is well behind you. In other words, the hook is set by the retrieve rather than a striking of the rod. Should the fish fail to become hooked, the lure will still be in place and you can continue to retrieve it a foot at a time. Quite often a fish that missed the first time will have a second go at it, or another fish will attack it. Only when you feel the fish hooked should you lift the rod so that the fish can be played.

It worked. The line went tight. I made the long retrieve and the fish was hooked. I then lifted the rod into a powerful fish which began to fight like mad, leaping then boring to the bottom, then shooting up and leaping again. Playing the fish was one thing, but landing it was something else as the bank was high above the water with sides covered in soft, slippery silt. I needed a hand and shouted as loud as I could, but Chris slept on. I did at last manage to guide the fish into a position where I was able to slip down the bank while getting covered in mud. No meal in the Anglers Arms now – on a cooler day I might have worn chest waders. But at last the fish was safely in the net, a real beauty weighing a little over 3lb. Had I been on my own I might well have returned the fish to the water, but Chris has five kids to feed and had so far failed to catch anything except a suntan. It would be a nice surprise for him when he finally woke up. His whole family enjoyed it the following day – with sauté potatoes and shrimp sauce. Chris is an engineer but he really should have been a chef.

Some time later I paid a visit to one of my favourite small estuaries in Argyll. This is a very clear estuary at times of low water and from where I stood on a narrow footbridge I could easily see a large head of sea trout shoaling on the sandy bottom, no doubt waiting for the next tide. I often fish from this footbridge, which is about forty yards wide, and once a fish is hooked it is easy to get down to the bank to play it. I was mindful that Emelio's Flattie lure (although he insists it's a crab lure) might work again here, so I put one on with a medium sinking line.

The majority of fish were lying in the middle of the river some ten yards below the bridge so, not wishing to disturb them in any way, I cast from the side of the bridge to a position beyond the shoal and once the line was lying along the bottom I slowly walked to the centre of the bridge, allowing the steady current to swing the line slowly round until it was running straight through the middle of the shoal. Fortunately the fish had not been unsettled by this, they simply moved out of the line's way then back into their original position. To them, it had probably appeared like some kind of stringy drifting weed. With the aid of polarised glasses I was able to see things in clear detail; I could even make out the lure now lying on the bottom a little way behind the shoal.

I began to retrieve in short, fast pulls – the current assisting the action by lifting the lure slightly with each pull and giving it a sort of bouncing action, which to me, at least, looked enticing, but would the fish think the same? As I worked it through the shoal, fish at the tail simply drifted to one side, but as it reached the head of the shoal it was suddenly taken and a lively fish bolted down the river. I wasted no time in getting down to the bank and followed the fish down the river, thankful that I was now able to play it some distance away from the rest of the shoal that, hopefully, had not been unsettled.

After landing a beautiful 2lb fish, I returned to the bridge half expecting the shoal to have gone. But they were still there. I repeated the same casting procedure and once the lure was in position I again started to retrieve. As the lure moved ever closer to the head of the shoal, where the fish had taken, a bee began to buzz a little too close to my face for comfort. The retrieve was halted while I shooed the pest away, and in that brief moment the lure settled on the river bed. When I resumed the retrieve – and I could see it as clear as a bell – a small cloud of sand kicked up. Quite obviously, the head chain eyes on the underside of the lure had caught

A

B

C

D

Instructions for the 'strip strike'. (A) With the rod pointing towards the lure and the line tension maintained with the first two fingers (in this case) of the right hand, the lure is retrieved in short, fast pulls, a foot or so at a time. (B) The take of a fish is felt as the lure is retrieved. (C) The retrieve is continued with a longer pull. (D) Only when the fish is felt to be hooked is the rod raised to play it.

The author with a fine 3lb sea trout caught on the lower reaches of the Cumbrian Leven. This fish was taken on the Little Flounder imitation as the river was falling following a small tide that had earlier backed the level up by no more than 3 or 4 inches.

in the river bed and caused a slight disturbance. The lure was immediately taken and another fish shot down the river. I wondered if this disturbance of the sand had acted as some kind of trigger, perhaps an indication of food, and as the shoal had still not been disturbed, I thought I might deliberately let the lure settle on the bottom and then give it a short, sharp tug. It worked again; as soon as the little cloud of sand kicked up the lure was grabbed immediately. Using the same method, I went on to take six more fish from the shoal before it was time to leave.

I thought that this might have been a one-off that had worked only on that particular day, as sea trout are not often caught in these clear and bright conditions. But I am reminded of a method that I have

often used to good effect when worming in slacker water, especially estuaries. The method is a simple one. Very often when the fish are not biting I reel in a foot or so, allowing the lead weight to cause a disturbance on the bottom. This often induces fish to take, particularly flat fish, but quite often it has produced a sea trout or two.

I can see the similarity to a crab in this lure because it has legs. I can also see a resemblance to small flounder in its flat body and tail. I saw a similar pattern in an American publication, which was called Mike's Velcro Crab. But here lies the theory of the curiosity factor; the lure is a little different from the norm, familiar yet curiously dissimilar, and must therefore be investigated. But whatever goes through the mind of a sea trout, this is a lure worth trying on tidal waters.

Little Flounder: The dressing

Hook	Size 1 Partridge Sea Prince saltwater fly hook
Silk	Strong pale olive to match the body. Use nylon sewing thread as an alternative
Tail	About six natural red cock hackle points with a few fine strands of metallic green Krystal Flash or similar mixed in
Body	Pale olive wired chenille, or pipe cleaner
Legs	Fine white rubber band with black markings at the tips
Eyes	4 mm bead chain in metal or plastic depending on the required weight

Notes: Wired chenille may not always be easy to obtain, in which case you might try dying some pipe cleaners. Alternatively, you could experiment by colouring the finished lure with a permanent marker.

This imitation of a little flounder (or is it a crab) has proved deadly for taking sea trout in tidal waters.

The heavier bead chain eyes will cause the lure to swim upside down, in other words with the hook up. There are two advantages to this. Firstly, because the lure is fished close to the bottom to imitate a small flounder it is less likely to get snagged. Secondly, a fish will almost certainly take the lure from above. The disadvantage of the heavy eyes is that it makes the lure hard to cast.

In some circumstances, as mentioned above, when fishing over a smooth silt or sandy bottom, the lure can be dragged slowly across the bottom for a short distance, allowing the eyes to scratch a disturbance. This will often induce a fish to investigate.

Construction

1   Fix the hook in the vice and wind on a bed of tying silk from the eye to the bend. (Whatever thread you use make sure that it is a strong one. Use nylon sewing thread even.) Select six natural red cock hackles and tie these in with the points pointing slightly outwards and away from the hook to form a tail that should be slightly longer than the body itself. The 'tail' hackles will flutter to give the lure a life-like movement. You can also tie in a few green metallic fibres, such as Krystal Flash, to give the lure that extra sparkle.

2   Return the thread to the eye of the hook and tie in the eyes tightly in a figure of eight on the upper side of the shank (Figure 30A).

3   Turn the hook over in the vice and tie

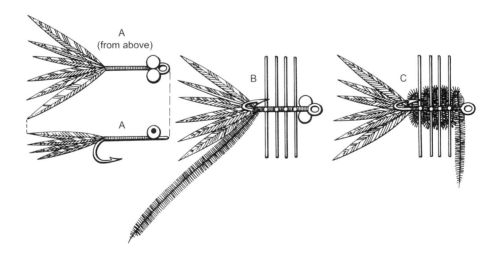

Figure 30. Construction of the Little Flounder. See text for instructions.

145

in four pairs of legs at equal distance along the shank. Do not tie the legs in with the tying thread as this will cut into the rubber. Simply knot them to the shank (Figure 30B). Do not snip the legs to length at this stage.

4 Catch in the wired chenille at the bend of the hook, then take the chenille back and across the hook shank in tight turns towards the eye while forming the flat body shape as you go. Tie the chenille down firmly each time you cross the shank (Figure 30C).

5 Tie the chenille down firmly behind the eye and snip off the excess.

6 Reverse the hook in the vice (hook upwards) and apply super glue to the whipping behind the eye and along the shank.

7 Snip the legs to length. They should protrude for about ½in beyond the body. To complete the lure, take a black permanent marker and touch the ends of the legs.

The lower beat of the River Clwyd in North Wales is a another good place to observe the influence of the tide. I have mentioned this river only as a typical example. The majority of rivers that I have fished, at least on the lower beats, conform in the same way.

This lower beat is called the Castle Beat due to the fact that it runs by Rhuddlan Castle. There are six major pools on this beat, starting with the Willow Pool that empties into the famous Barrier Pool. Below this is Bishops Pool, followed by Abbey Pool, then the Landslide Pool, then the bottom pool – Castle Pool. The river then runs straight for a quarter of a mile before running under Rhuddlan Bridge and on for three more miles before it spills into the sea at Rhyl.

Fishing the Castle Beat with its pools, glides and rapids is not very different from fishing on higher reaches of the river – until the tide comes in. You can be busy fishing without realising that the pools have risen a few inches – or more on a big tide. The

The Willow Pool on the Castle Beat of the River Clwyd. Here the level is affected by the tide. The shingle on the right of the picture was under water fifteen minutes before this picture was taken.

Fishing for sea trout on the estuary of the River Erne, Ballyshannon.

problem now is that far too many sea trout running up on the top of the tide continue to push up through the Castle Beat until they arrive at the Junction Pool a little further upstream. This is a pool that seems to draw fish like a magnet, but beyond the pocket of a writer I'm afraid. Fortunately, this extra height does not last for long, sometimes only for as long as fifteen minutes, before it starts to drop again. But while it is dropping, causing the speed of the current to pick up and the fish to slow down, you can expect to hit one of the bigger sea trout that frequent this river and which didn't quite make it as far as the Junction Pool.

If you were to wait along the straight section between Rhuddlan Bridge and the Castle Pool, when the tide begins to back the river up you will often see the torpedo-like bow waves made by the bigger fish as they head upstream. I have tried casting in front of them on many occasions but so far without success. It can be very frustrating. The river below Rhuddlan Bridge is rarely fished except by a few who fish for flounders and eels, although when the tide is out a good many likely streamy runs are revealed in which sea trout lie. This is free fishing, the only requirement being a rod licence.

Estuaries can be a mile wide or very narrow, while some rivers have no estuary at all. In rugged mountainous areas they might tumble straight into the sea from the rocky shore. I can think of numerous other small rivers that have no estuary as such – they simply run across the beach, similar to the small stream that I am familiar with in North Wales where some big sea trout can be caught at low tide.

A fine sea trout from the estuary shore of the River Erne, Ballyshannon.

147

This stream runs swiftly off the hillside before falling over a high man-made stone wall onto a beach littered with rocks and pebbles. It runs over the beach for little more than 100 yards before entering the sea by some docks. Because fish are unable to get beyond the wall, they will run up to it, hang about for a while, then turn back. But this is something you will only see at low water as the tide rises as far as the wall itself.

I first discovered this spot while on holiday some years ago. I love boats and everything about them. So on this particular night, after buying fish and chips, I

Russell Whiteman with a lovely sea trout from the estuary shore, River Ray, Co Donegal.

decided to eat them along the dock wall. It was dark by then and as I sat eating my supper a security light on the opposite side of the stream was turned on. Caught in the light were about twenty big sea trout slowly making their way up the stream.

It was an hour later when I returned with my fishing tackle, but by then the tide had come in and covered the stream as though it had never existed. The following night I was ready and in that short length of stream, which was no more than a foot deep, I took four sea trout between 2 and 4lb on a small Medicine before the tide came in to spoil the fun. I have returned to this place on a number of occasions since and have never failed to catch sea trout. You will forgive me if I do not mention where it is, as I doubt if even the locals know about it.

There was another occasion when my wife and I took our six grandchildren to Anglesey for a short break. One particular night as we were taking a walk along the sandy beach near Moelfre we arrived at a stream, barely more than a trickle, which ran out of the dunes and over the beach. We could easily have paddled through it but a few yards upstream amongst the dunes was a little wooden foot-bridge. Jessica, forever the explorer, went on ahead to cross it and as she reached the centre of it I saw her begin to wave her arms excitedly. I caught up to see what all the excitement was about. There, in the small pool beneath the bridge, was a shoal of about fifty sea trout that averaged about three quarters of a pound in weight.

I have often thought about returning to this stream, especially after a good downpour of rain, which might encourage a few bigger fish into it, but so far I have not had the opportunity. There are only a handful of small rivers on Anglesey where sea trout can be caught, but the fishing around the coast can be excellent once you know

Sea trout fishing along the estuary of the River Erne, Ballyshannon.

where to go. My friend Chris Slater regularly fishes for sea trout along this part of the coast, and with success too.

Anyone who has ever had the pleasure of reading that wonderful book *Sea Trout Run* by Peter Jarrams might recall the cover, which is of an angler fishing the outlet of a small river that enters Loch Eil with Ben Nevis in the background. That angler, you might be interested to know, is myself.

This tiny river enters the loch at its very end beyond Kinlocheil and it is here that I have had some excellent sea trout fishing over the years. At low tide the mouth of the river is probably less than fifteen yards wide and not more than three feet at its deepest. Its edges are surrounded by slippery rocks covered in bladderwrack, so one has to take some care in getting into a fishable position, but the effort is well worth it.

I discovered this stream quite by chance many years ago while on a caravan holiday near Fort William in August. As ever, I was in search of some sea trout fishing and thought it would be a good idea to take a look at Loch Eilt, which was about twenty miles up the road on the way to Mallaig. I had heard much about Loch Eilt. In those

Fishing an ebbing tide on the shore of Donegal.

days it used to be an excellent sea trout loch and noted for its genuine run of spring sea trout. Unfortunately, this loch seems to have declined in recent years, probably due to the salmon farming operations in Loch Ailort into which the river that flows from Loch Eilt enters. This, alas, seems to be a common problem in the Scottish sea lochs and I think that the appropriate authorities should do something about it. But I suppose that there is big money in salmon farming and the lobby that seeks to protect its interests is a powerful one. The pollution caused by salmon farming can only be described as a disgrace, and the food that farmed salmon are fed on is another matter of contention.

I never did get as far as Loch Eilt on that particular occasion. As I passed by the top end of Loch Eil (I apologise for the similarity in the spelling of these two lochs) I caught sight of a small stream that enters there, a stream I might not have noticed had the tide been in. I paid little heed to it and continued up the road. But something beckoned me to fish that stream, something that shouted sea trout. I turned back.

I parked the car, tackled up and picked my way through the rocks and weed until I was in a reasonable position to be able to cast into the narrow channel between the bladderwrack. I was using a floating line and, if I remember correctly, the fly was a small Peter Ross that was grabbed immediately by a small herling – a juvenile sea trout. The second cast produced another herling and on it went, one small herling after the other. In the absence of anything bigger, I thought I might have some fun float fishing for these herling so I returned to the car and got out my son's float rod. Unfortunately, I was without any bait as I had left a tin of worms under the caravan to keep them cool. Not being deterred, I plucked a few winkles from the rocks and put one of these on. The herling liked the

winkles just as much as the fly I had been using and for the next hour, or more, I had great fun. The act of watching the float bob under and striking into a fish, albeit a small one, was exhilarating – almost like being a young boy all over again. Although this was great fun, it was adult sea trout that I really wished to catch. It seemed that my instinct had proved me wrong; perhaps all I would ever catch here was herling. I returned to the caravan park for dinner.

Later in the evening I still had that little river on my mind. Would sea trout enter it after dark? High tide was not due until two in the morning so I still had plenty of time to find out. And so, after bribing my wife with a novel, which I bought from the camp shop, and promising to take her and the kids to Loch Ness the following day, I was on my way back up the road.

The first hour between dusk and darkness produced yet more small herling. I was beginning to feel a little guilty about being here when I should have been spending the time with my family. Then, just as I had decided to pack up and go, a fish swirled at the fly and missed it. Guilty feelings of selfishness and self-indulgence went out of my head. Fish were here. Sea trout! A few minutes later the line went tight and a fine fish bolted towards the expanse of the loch. This was what I had come for. I just knew I would catch sea trout here.

The fish was fighting hard, as sea trout caught in tidal waters do, and I had to employ every bit of skill and experience to play him back through the weed. It was a fit fish, which at first I imagined to be at least 4lb, or even more. But it wasn't; it weighed a little less than 2lb, but what a beautiful silver sea-liced fish it was. I went on to take four more sea trout, all around the same weight, and lost one that was much bigger. But now the tide had started to come in. Had I really been here this long? It was time to make tracks and think of a way of getting

A good position from which to fish for sea trout. They run close to this rocky outcrop.

back to the caravan without disturbing the rest of the campers – or my wife and two young children for that matter.

I have returned to this stream whenever I have had the opportunity and have always had sport in the night when tides permitted.

ALONG THE SHORE

Fishing in salt water along the shore can be very rewarding, although it is not the most popular branch of the sport and is only

Loch Creran on the west coast of Scotland. The ideal shore to fish for sea trout.

151

practised by a small number of dedicated sea trout anglers. There are some well-known salt water venues where sea trout are caught with regularity, such as the Voes of Shetland and along the rugged coast of Donegal in the northwest of Ireland. However, sea trout can be caught almost anywhere along the coast of Ireland, Scotland, the Scottish Islands, Wales, the north, the northeast and the southwest of England. In other word they can be caught in every region where sea trout rivers enter the sea. Sea trout in search of any particular river travel along the coast where they feed avidly on sand eels and other small shoaling fish. It is reasonable to assume that if you are anywhere within ten or so miles of the mouth of such a river then you will be in with a good chance.

But exactly where should one begin? There are few clues to be had from sea anglers who fish with lug and ragworm and other concoctions attached to booms and great lumps of lead. Sea trout are cautious fish and will not look at such baits or tackle. Local knowledge is useful and it is a good idea to make a few enquiries in the local tackle shop. On the other hand, some of the best saltwater fishing is that which I have found for myself. I always look for the shores that are stony and weedy and not too deep. Much like bass, sea trout like to travel in shallower water, fifteen feet at the most where this is possible, and I have often caught them in less than a foot of water. Seek out the shores that are strewn with weed and boulders; these are the places where sea trout like to feed. Look out for the likely places where the fish might lie in wait to ambush a meal. Where the current is forced to race between rocks or over shallow reefs or even old sewage pipes are likely places to catch sea trout.

The best time to catch sea trout will be when the tide is ebbing and the weed is flowing and snaking in the current. On a rising tide, sea trout tend to move on much as they would in a rising river, but when the tide is on the ebb they will hang about and continue to feed until the height of water is sometimes less than a foot deep. I like to follow the tide out, wading and casting into the channels between the weed or seeking out likely places between the rocks.

Dawn on a Scottish sea loch. Sea trout were feeding close in amongst the weed as this picture was taken.

A Snake Fly or something similar that represents a sand eel fished on a floating or intermediate line usually works best. I was recently given a lure by Chris Slater, who is the bailiff on the upper River Leven in Cumbria. Chris is an expert at catching sea trout, both in fresh and salt water, and I am assured that this one has accounted for a good many sea trout, especially along the Anglesey coast. This is a type of Snake Fly dressing, the difference being that Chris dresses his on a mount of doubled 10lb BS nylon that forms a loop for the eye. However, for ease, the construction of the mount can be the same as given earlier in the book for the Snake Fly, either in the original dressing or in Paul Hopwood's braided mount dressing. Chris is a great believer in dressing his saltwater lures long, even as long as 5in. It also uses more winging material than the Snake Fly and has a false hackle and cheeks.

The dressing

Mount	Same as Snake Fly
Hooks	Size 14–8 depending on length
Body	Fine holographic Mylar tubing
Wing	First a few strands of pearl Krystal Flash. Above this is goat hair dyed light blue. Over this is green pearl Flashabou
Beard	White Arctic fox
Cheeks	Jungle cock

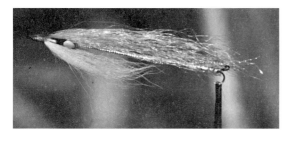

Chris Slater's Salt Water Lure.

Head	Green
Length	3–5in

Not long ago on a hot, late August afternoon I travelled down the Mull of Kintyre on my way to Campbeltown. This is one of the most beautiful coastal routes in the world; the scenery is simply spectacular. It's a long climb over the Rest And Be Thankful from Loch Long to the northern end of Loch Fyne. But there was little traffic on the road and I was soon passing through the beautiful town of Inverary, then along the shore of Loch Fyne through the villages of Furnace and Minard and on to the little town of Lochgilphead where the A83 joins the A816 from Oban. All along this coast there are opportunities to fish for sea trout from the shore. Once, Loch Fyne was famous for its quality of sea trout fishing and was one of the best sea lochs in the whole of Scotland. The favourite method of catching them was with a thin strip of mackerel that, I'm sure, was taken for a sand eel. The Snake Fly and similar lures are now becoming more popular and replacing the need for such messy, if not smelly, baits.

Unfortunately, over the last twenty-five years or so all forms of fishing, including sea trout fishing, on Loch Fyne have declined. This is thought to be due to the salmon farming activities along its coastline. In addition to this, because of fish stock restrictions, instead of heading out to sea, trawlers have been netting right up to the head of the loch for langoustine, squat lobster, and anything else that comes their way. The creelers, who are known for their conservation practice, have had their lines cut on countless occasions over the past few years by these trawlers, which sweep up the loch without respect for anything or anyone and with total disregard for the ecological consequences. A number of cases have been brought before the court. Some have been lost on technicalities and one or

153

Low water on a Scottish sea loch.
A perfect fly fishing location.

Days of plenty. Before the days of salmon farming,
catches like this were common along the shore of Loch
Fyne and in its feeder rivers such as the River Aray, the
River Fyne and the River Douglas.

two have been won or settled out of court. It is hoped that the newly formed Scottish Creelers and Divers Association (SCAD) will continue to make headway in its fight against the perpetrators and that one day we will see this beautiful loch restored to its former glory. Perhaps there is a lesson to be learned from the Loch Torridon experiment, where the loch was declared a conservation area and trawling is no longer allowed. This has been a very successful exercise and long may it continue to be so.

Back on the road again. From Lochgilphead I continued along the shore of Loch Fyne and on to Tarbert where the road crosses the Mull and continues along the shore of West Loch Tarbert and the Sound of Gigha. Here the view across the sea to Islay is awe inspiring. The late afternoon sun was still burning down and even with all the windows open it was becoming unbearable, so before reaching Glenacardoch Point I pulled in at the side of the road to take a long drink of warm, and now flat, lemonade.

Just a short distance out from the road I noticed a small group of tiny islands on which a large colony of seals were basking in the sun. Every now and again one or two seals would slip into the water and swim about for a short distance before hauling themselves back onto the rocks. I got the impression that they were not doing this to cool down, rather that they were feeding. This was confirmed when one came up with a fish in its mouth. I guessed that there must be a shoal of mackerel about and, as I had some time to spare, I decided that I would spend the next hour or so fishing for them. By then it would be more bearable to continue driving.

I tackled up my fly rod with a floating line and a small Snake Fly. No waders on this occasion. It was far too hot. The shorts and trainers I was already wearing would be fine. The seals seemed completely oblivious to the idiot who was now wading out amongst the kelp, but all the same I thought it wise to keep a reasonable distance from them. Before me was a narrow channel between the weed into which I cast. Almost as soon as I began to retrieve I had a hard take and the fish began to run. At first I thought it must be a bigger than average mackerel, but this was a strong fish that I dared to hope might even be a sea trout. It was – a lovely silver fish weighing about 2lb. The second cast produced another sea trout of a similar weight. I took around twenty sea trout over the course of the next two hours with an average weight of 1½lb. All were returned.

The following day, on my way back, I stopped again by the little islands. But this time the tide was in and I didn't have much luck, at least not with sea trout. I did, however, receive a consolation prize of two mackerel and a saith, known in England as a coalfish.

There are countless places along the coast where it is possible to catch sea trout, many of which are yet to be discovered simply because no one has ever bothered to fish for them. I was once driving to Anglesey to meet up with a couple of mates to do a spot of sea fishing. But I didn't have any bait and, not wanting to be regarded as a scrounger, I decided it would be a good idea to take a fork and stop along the way to dig some lug worm. I had previously passed a place that had looked likely. I turned off the main road and down a narrow lane that lead to a muddy shore where tufts of seaweed grew at intervals amongst the mud and countless tiny creeks. It was low tide so the digging was easy and I soon had enough worms to last me for the day.

As I made my way back to the car along the high water line, I met a man coming towards me who, as it happened, was also intent on digging some bait. He was a rotund man in his mid-thirties. He eyed me with an intimidating frown, which suggested that I wasn't particularly welcome. Nevertheless, we struck up a form of reluctant conversation from which I gathered he lived not a mile away and was a professional bait digger, although the exercise of digging hadn't done much for his waistline. His somewhat aggressive manner suggested that he wasn't too pleased to see this invader on the beach that he obviously considered as his own private domain. I felt obliged to explain that I was only digging enough worms to last me for the rest of the day and that I was not intent on selling them. His surly attitude ebbed slightly at this and as the mostly one-sided conversation continued and the know-it-all began to brag about what a great fisherman he was, he happened to mention that the previous day he had noticed fish moving amongst the weeds at low tide. He hadn't bothered fishing for them – only mullet – and he didn't fancy fishing for something that was almost impossible to catch. My ears pricked up. Could it be possible? By good luck my fly tackle was in the car, so I phoned my friends on my mobile and told them that I might be a little late.

Can you spot the difference? A real sand eel and an imitation. Lures, such as the Snake fly, which represent a sand eel can be deadly in salt water.

When I returned a few minutes later, the bait digger was shaking his head in mock pity. 'You must be mad, mate,' he sneered, sticking his fork in the mud. 'You wont catch mullet on that. You need bread for them, and you still wont catch bugger all.' Undeterred, I waded into the shallow water and began to cast here and there amongst the weeds, while the digger-man stood leaning on his fork, smirking. I turned towards him, shrugged, and gave him an incongruous smile.

'You must be bloody mad, you,' he reminded me again.

I was hoping the idiot's fork would snap under his bulk and he would fall face down in the mud, but no such luck. I cast again towards a large clump of weed and began a slow retrieve. Suddenly I got a take. A fish was on and the reel was screaming as it rushed out towards the open sea. There was no mistake, this was a sea trout and a good one too. It was putting up a terrific fight. Next, it boiled on the surface then again made off, running hard and fast. But my luck held and after a while I managed to steer it back through the weeds until I was able to slip the net under it. It was a fabulous silver fish, which I estimated was a little under 5lb.

That wiped the smirk off his face. The tide was on its way in now and it was time to go. 'See you,' I said as I walked past him carrying my prize. He made no reply but I did hear him grunt something when I was a little way past him. I couldn't quite make out what he had said, but I'm sure it began with a 'b'.

17   Out on the Loch

When we think of sea trout lochs of the freshwater kind, the first that come to mind might be the more famous ones, such as Loch Maree, Loch Stack or Loch Lomond. Then there are the lochs of Hebridean Isles or the loughs of Ireland, such as Lough Currane and Lake Caragh, to name but a few. Equally, there are countless small lochs and lochans, some of which are hardly ever fished, which can also offer excellent sport when conditions are favourable. So what makes for a good sea trout loch and what are the best conditions for fly fishing?

No loch will be worth fishing unless enough water is flowing out of it to encourage fish to run up the river. Regular intervals of rain will bring up a regular supply of fresh fish, although some lochs that have a large river flowing from them may be less dependent on rain than others. All good sea trout lochs have one thing in common – a short river that flows between them and the sea. The best sport will be with fresh fish that have not had too far to run and are still fresh when entering the loch. The longer a fish is in the loch, and river too for that matter, the harder they will be to catch. My advice is to take a look at the river before fishing the loch.

Sea trout favour lochs with rocky shores and islands and shallower margins. It also helps if there are a number of burns entering, in which they will later spawn. Depths of between ten and fifteen feet are usually good sea trout holding areas. Weather can also play a large part. A hot day under a bright, clear blue sky when the surface is flat calm is never a good time to fish on any

Intermittent cloud and a good wave. What more could a loch fisherman ask for?

kind of still water, whether it be loch, lake or reservoir. Fish are not very enthusiastic about looking upwards for surface food on days like these and even a fly fished deep can often be unrewarding. You might just as well spend some time on the beach, or a beer garden, and wait until the evening when there is less glare in the sky. The best days are those when a steady westerly wind is blowing and creating a wave height of about six inches; better still if there is cloud cover with the sun breaking through intermittently.

Times of the tide should also be a consideration. As strange as it might seem, the best time to fish a loch is one hour before and one hour after high tide. There is something in the metabolism of sea trout that makes them feed with more intensity at these times. Even when a loch is some distance from the sea, this peak taking time can still take place.

I hope that the above information will be of some help, although I do appreciate that my description of a sea trout loch has been brief. However, this book is about flies and fly fishing and not the natural history of lochs. So let's go fishing.

Loch fishing has a magic all of its own. Oh to be afloat on a day when dark dramatic clouds roll across the sky, casting shadows over the hills in ever-changing hues. This could inspire one to put aside his rod for a while and take up paints and canvas in the almost impossible hope of capturing, if only for a moment, the majesty of the scene. An eagle soars high above and a fresh wind ruffles the surface of the water, carrying the boat ever closer towards the drift where sea trout are known to take. Anticipation runs high. Waves lap at the boat's hull, laughing and gurgling. 'Here' says the boatman and the long rod is raised for the wind to catch the line and carry the dancing fly tantalisingly over the surface. A fish newly up from the sea swirls as it takes, leaving a calm circle amongst the waves, and runs tearing line from the reel. It leaps and nerves tingle as a silent prayer is offered that the hook will hold. Such is the thrill of loch fishing.

When I lived in Ayrshire I would often fish Loch Eck. This loch, which is seven miles long and hardly more than three-quarters of a mile wide at any point, is one of the most beautiful places in Scotland. Surrounded by forests and hills and rich in wildlife, to me it is, and always will be, a special place. From this loch flows the wonderful little River Echaig, a noted salmon and sea trout stream, which enters the sea

(Left) A fighting fit sea trout safely in the net, Lough Fermoyle, Conemara. It was on this lough that Mr Justice Kingsmill Moore developed his Bumble dapping flies. (Right) And safely in the boat.

Fishing a good drift on Lough Fermoyle, Conemara.

at Holy Loch and which I have also been privileged to fish on many occasions. I can think of a number of times when I fished Loch Eck and caught nothing. Although, thinking about it, these were probably days when conditions were not favourable for sea trouting; they were balmy summer days when the surface was like a mill pond and fish were dour. Nevertheless, it was nice just to be there and occasionally try for the odd brown trout or two. However, there was one particular day at the end of August that I will never forget.

The wind was getting up a bit as I crossed on the car ferry from Gourock to Dunoon. The boat was rocking and it was not the most comfortable of crossings. The thought crossed my mind that if the wind grew any stronger no boats would be allowed out on the loch. Then again, perhaps the hills that surrounded it would provide some shelter and the wind would be less fierce than it was here on the Clyde. The boat docked and I drove out of Dunoon towards Ardbeg, passing Holy Loch to my right where nuclear submarines berthed like giant blue whales. I crossed the River Echaig and was encouraged to see that there was plenty of

water coming down. Surely fish would be running up to the loch in this, but I still wasn't sure if boats would be available, or if boating would be a good idea in this wind, which was now reaching gale force. The consolation, however, was the river that I would fish if I couldn't get a boat. I turned the radio on. The Sex Pistols immediately assaulted my ears with their grinding rendition of *God Save the Queen*. I tried changing stations but all I got was more Punk. I turned it off. Give me the Beatles, Frank Sinatra or Ella Fitzgerald any day, or even some classical on occasions. I continued through Strath Fachaig with the Echaig running high on the left-hand side of the road until, at last, I arrived at Loch Eck. The wind from the southwest was subdued by the hills and a choppy six-inch wave churned the surface. Perfect. I called in at the Whistlefield Inn where I paid for the boat and was told that an angler who had been out earlier had taken a decent bag of sea trout and two salmon. I couldn't get out quick enough.

With the assistance of a boatman, loch fishing is made much easier because the angler can concentrate on his fishing instead of concerning himself with the constant handling of the boat. But there are times when I prefer to be alone and not under the supervision, imagined or otherwise, of someone who prefers me to fish according to his instructions. I often enjoy my own company. Out on the loch I become a passenger on the wind. However, although I probably catch less fish than I would under the supervision of such an expert, I remain my own master and if I hit upon a mark, or a method that yields fish, I then have the satisfaction of having discovered something new for myself. I can think of at least three occasions when a boatman was employed and I caught very little. Only when I insisted on fishing drifts based on my own intuition and experience of 'reading' the water, did I hit upon fish.

Broadside on to the wind, the boat was still being pushed faster than I really wanted to travel. Fortunately I had brought a drogue along, which I attached to the rowlock. Soon I was moving at a pace that suited me. With the wind behind me, and drifting some fifty yards out parallel with the roadside, I was nearing a shingle spit where I had taken sea trout the previous year. I saw no reason why a particular technique I had used on that occasion should not work again. This had involved using a slow-sinking line and a single fly, which had been a Silver Invicta dressed on a size 8 hook. As much as I like the excitement of fishing the fly on, or close to, the surface, the advantage, if advantage is the word, of fishing a sunken fly is that I do not see the fish take – I only feel it. All too often when a fish boils at a fly on the surface, the temptation, unless you have nerves of steel, is to strike immediately and often the fish is missed and the proverbial curse is uttered about short takers. At least when fishing deeper I have no knowledge of whether a fish has come frustratingly short of the fly or not. I continue to fish in the normal manner until

I feel the fish actually take and then lift the rod into it in the almost certainty that he will be hooked.

The Silver Invicta was tied on. To have cast towards the bank would not have been a good idea as reeds grew along this part of the shore and any fish hooked would only make a dash for them and disappointment would be certain to follow. I was almost over the shingle spit now as I cast to my left at right angles to the boat. It is, of course, easier to cast at right angles to the wind rather than trying to cast into it. As the boat pushed forward on the wind the line began to swing round in an arc, accelerating slightly in its track until it was fishing directly behind the boat. It is while the line swings in this arc that you will often get a take, and usually from a bigger fish. Once the line is running straight, it is time to start the retrieve in short, steady pulls until it is time to cast again. The retrieve should be slow and relative to the speed that the boat is moving at. Too fast and the fly will travel at a speed that would be impossible for a natural creature of the same size to swim at and will appear suspicious. You might for a while let the wind do the work for you by not retrieving and letting the fly trail behind the boat. If the boat is rolling on the waves, another good trick is to touch the rod down on the side of the boat pointing slightly upwards so that the rolling action causes the fly to jerk in the deadly form of sink and draw. I have taken many sea trout by doing this, but it can be tempting to leave the rod resting over the side of the boat while you light a cigarette or have a drink from your flask. So if you must leave go of the rod for any reason, make sure that the butt is resting on the seat with the reel handle pointing upwards. This way, if a fish takes the reel will spin freely. You should also make sure that the clutch is not too tight or it might be the last you will see of your rod should a salmon or big sea trout make off with the fly. This happened to a close friend when fishing on Loch Maree and an expensive lesson was learned. A further tip when 'resting' the rod is to pull a loop of the line and place it under a weight on the seat so that, in that brief second when a fish takes, the weight will set the hook before the line is pulled from under it. An old friend of mine made good use of a tobacco tin into which he had poured molten lead. A hole was then drilled through the corner of the tin through which was tied a length of cord. The cord was then tied to the boat seat, but not so long that if it fell it would clatter on the bottom or the side of the boat.

Fishing behind a drifting boat is sometimes regarded as trolling and may be frowned upon by some, especially on stocked waters. I disagree with this opinion. As far as I'm concerned, trolling is towing a lure such as a Toby, or something similar, behind a boat that is powered by an outboard motor operated by the angler or a second party. A lazy man's, if not a fishmonger's, way of fishing. Many years ago I tried trolling for salmon on Lough

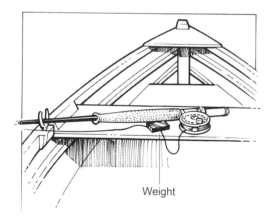

Weight

Figure 31. When resting the rod it is a good idea to place a weight on the line. If a fish takes, the weight will set the hook before the line is pulled from under it. The weight should also be tied to the boat seat to prevent it falling with a bang on the bottom of the boat.

Melvin over on the west coast of Ireland. In the course of six hours I took over twenty salmon and killed one. I have never tried it since as I decided then that this method of fishing was unsporting. However, fishing a fly behind a boat quietly drifting on the wind is not quite the same thing. I will also add that if the boat was anchored while the line was retrieved it would not be considered as trolling, no matter which way you cast, either up- or downwind. The only difference is that in a drifting boat you are covering more water.

With the aid of a boatman, it would have been an easy matter to fish a method known as 'crosswind fishing'. This way the boat is rowed at right angles to the wind with the bow pointing slightly into the wind. This helps to maintain the direction. The angler then casts downwind and the line swings round as the boat moves forward. Once the line is directly astern, the angler starts to retrieve the fly. This is a highly successful way of fishing, although an impossible operation when fishing alone.

Fishing ahead of a drifting boat using a floating line, such as when fishing traditional loch style with a team of two or three flies, or when dibbling or dapping, which I will deal with later, can be both exciting and rewarding. But for now we are fishing behind the boat. Some are of the opinion that this is not a good method because you are fishing water over which the boat has passed. To me this seems to make little difference. If you were foolish enough to make a loud noise or drop some heavy item in the bottom of the boat then, without doubt, the fish would be scared away. But a boat that drifts quietly over the lies, in my own experience, never does any harm and fish are just as likely to be taken behind the boat as they would in front of it.

When fishing behind a drifting boat, either with a sinking or a floating line, the same zig-zag method described under

Perfect conditions on a small Scottish loch. At the time this picture was taken the river was in spate and the loch was full of fresh sea trout.

'The Medicine' can be put to good use. The principle is the same, only this time, assuming that the boat is drifting broadside on to the wind, the angler might start by pointing the rod first towards the bow then slowly bringing it round towards the stern. Instead of moving in a straight line, the fly now follows a snaking track and covers more water.

The line was swinging round and almost in a direct line behind the boat when I got a hard take that bent the rod well over. I felt that it was a heavy fish as it bored towards the middle of the loch. So I let it run, applying only the minimum of pressure. Before I knew it I was on the backing with the fish still running hard and fast. It was then that I wished I had a boatman with me who could row after it before the backing line ran out. Fortunately, the fish turned and headed back towards the boat, which had now bumped up on the shore amongst the reeds. I took a chance, grabbed the anchor and threw it up the shore before scrambling out. I waded along the bank a short distance to where no reeds grew and where, if I was lucky, I might be able to play and land my fish, which was still fighting

with considerable power. It swirled and I saw that it was not a sea trout but a salmon, a nice one of perhaps 10 or even 12lb. Even on a dark day such as this one, people seem to emerge from nowhere and soon I had an audience of holidaymakers. Ramblers, mums pushing babies in prams, grandparents and favourite aunties all assembled behind me to watch the show that, in these parts, was possibly the most exciting thing they had seen all week. Now they would have something to talk about when they got home. I didn't wish to make a fool of myself and played the fish with as much care as possible until at last, and to much applause from the crowd, which caused me some considerable embarrassment, the fish was netted.

That was a good start to the day, but I still fancied catching a sea trout and thought it would now be a good opportunity to change tactics.

Dibbling

Soon I was back in the boat, but this time I was going to have a go at dibbling. Some have other names for this method of fishing

A well hackled Bibio. This is a great fly for dibbling, and in larger sizes it is also a good dappling fly.

but this is the word that I have always used and I see no reason for changing it now. I hardly ever use a dropper when fishing a river, but on a loch the dropper can serve a useful purpose and it is the fly that sea trout are usually taken on. For this method, I use a floating line and a three-yard cast. The point fly consists of something more traditional, such as a size 10 or 12 Mallard and Claret, while the dropper, or 'bob fly' as it is known, some three feet away is a little bushier and is less likely to get drowned. A Zulu or any similar well-hackled fly usually does the trick, but in more recent years I have found that a Hackled Silver Bibio, well soaked in Permafloat and dressed on a size 10 medium shank hook, works best. The point fly only serves as a weight at the end of the cast and as it is less air resistant and slightly heavier than the bob it assists the casting. The method is to cast in any direction away from the boat and dibble the bob fly across the surface. Casting ahead of a drifting boat with a short line in the traditional fashion, and raising the rod to make the bob fly skip the surface, is perhaps the most successful way of dibbling. However,

I have caught a good many sea trout when casting a long line, even behind the boat.

The wind was abating a little as the afternoon drew on, but there was still enough breeze to create a good fishing wave, a wave that was perfect for dibbling. The boat was now nearing the top end of the loch where the River Cur enters and where I was confident of taking a sea trout or two. Ahead of me a sea trout boiled on the surface. What, if anything, it had taken I did not know, but there was every chance of it coming again at something that was tempting enough. Even with the aid of the drogue the boat was still drifting a little too fast and by the time I had put up the line I had drifted past the spot where the fish had boiled. The boil mark was still visible, but now I found myself casting behind the boat, which drifted on trailing the line and flies behind it. When I judged that the flies were over where the fish had shown, I raised the rod. This made the bob fly skitter over the surface. A fish boiled at the fly; I struck and missed. How many times had this happened? That sudden burst of adrenaline that makes one react too quickly. I should have known better than to strike at the rise, but I am not super-human and to this day I occasionally make the same mistake when my senses are honed.

I continued casting and dibbling the bob fly in front of the boat without any giveaway signs from a rising fish. Then suddenly a fish broke the surface and chased the bob fly, a Hackled Silver Bibio, for about two feet, took and turned in a dive to the bottom. I hadn't seen many sea trout take in quite this way before; rainbow trout, yes, but rarely sea trout. I was wondering if it was a sea trout at all. But it was, and after putting up a good scrap I eventually leaned over the side and the net was under it. It was a beautiful fresh fish of about 2lb that was still sea liced and had probably only just come up the river. Three more

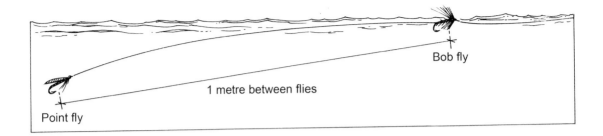

Figure 32. Dibbling. *The hackled bob fly, which is treated with floatant, is 'dibbled' across the surface. It is usually the bob fly which is taken; the point fly acts as a weight at the end of the leader.*

sea trout were taken that afternoon by dibbling, but I had intended to try my hand at dapping at some point in the day. But first I would have to return to my car and get out the rod for the purpose.

Dapping

Dapping, then, provides a most thrilling experience with each and every fish, it attracts the big ones better than any other method, and it requires a very special skill of its own. It also requires nerves of iron and at times an almost superhuman degree of self-control. What more can an angler wish for?

Jock Scott
Sea Trout Fishing, 1969

This form of fly fishing, which uses a blow-line to carry a bushy fly on the wind, is said to have originated on Loch Maree in the mid-1930s. However, the general concept is much older. On the Irish loughs the idea of using a natural mayfly to be carried on the wind to gorging trout has been in use for centuries.

For dapping you will need a long rod with stand-off rings, which will help to dry

Dibbling on Lough Fermoyle, Conemara.

164

A fresh sea trout from Loch Voshimid, Isle of Harris, Outer Hebrides. (Courtesy of Arthur Oglesby.)

A Blue Zulu dapping fly.

off the blow-line, particularly if you use a floss line or after a fish has been played and the line has received a good soaking. I use a 15ft float rod, which was given to me by a keen match fisherman. Because I like to use a fly reel the reel seat position has been moved to the butt end. Some anglers prefer to use a fixed spool reel or even a multiplier, but I think a fly reel with a large arbour does best.

The blow-line is an essential part of the dapper's armoury. A good blow-line should be light and strong with a good enough sail area. Some leading fishing tackle suppliers stock blow-lines that are made from floss nylon, which will dry out quicker than other materials. I once tried using floss silk of the kind used in fly dressing. This had a limited success, but the best I ever came across was an idea given to me by my old mate John Wilshaw. Here's how to make it.

Take two large nails and cut off the flat heads. Knock each nail into a fence post so that they are about ten yards apart. Using a spool of 2lb BS nylon, tie the end to one of the nails, pay off the line and take it round the second nail then back again. Keep winding the line round the nails until you

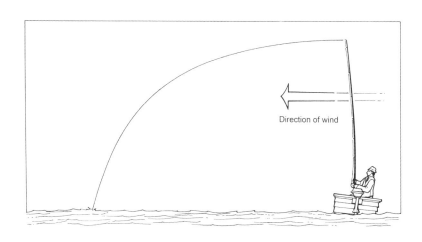

Direction of wind

Figure 33. Dapping. Good use is made of the wind to make the dapping fly dance and trip along the surface. With a little practice the angler can make the fly perform in a tantalising manner.

have completed about twenty turns. Slide the nylon away from one of the nails while maintaining a tension against the other nail. Tie a simple overhand knot every 18in along the length of nylon until you reach the other nail. The easiest way to do this is to coil the line up as you go rather than try pulling the entire length of the line through each knot. And there you have it, an excellent blow-line that will carry well on the wind and needs little, if any, drying out after being submerged.

Because we need to maintain a certain amount of control over the fly, its movement, and its direction of travel, it is best that the leader is a short one. My own choice is a 3ft leader of 8lb BS.

The choice of dapping flies is endless. At one time, one of the most popular flies was the Loch Ordie, a big bushy fly with a dangling treble that was thought to tackle short takers. But such flies are rarely used these days. Bumble flies, the creation of the famous Mr Justice Kingsmill Moore and author of *A Man May Fish* are still popular. Having a resemblance to a large bumble bee in as much as the mixed hackles give the fly a striped appearance, it is obvious why they are called Bumbles. There is no set pattern to this fly, it is the style rather than dressing that leaves room for the fly dresser to create his own Bumble patterns. Below I give you one of my own favourite dressings, although I make no claim that it works better than any other similar dressing.

Jim's Bumble Fly

Hooks	Size 4, 6 or 8 Partridge single low water
Silk	Black
Tail	Brown bucktail
Body	No body materials are used as the hackles cover the entire body
Hackles	1st hackle (starting at the bend of the hook). Cock hackle dyed black
	2nd hackle. A light blue cock hackle
	3rd hackle. Black cock same as first
	4th hackle. A cock hackle dyed bright red
Rib	Fine silver wire wound between the hackles
Head	Black

Other similar dapping flies are featured in the colour section.

Here's another good dapping fly you might like to dress. It is a pattern given to me many years ago by Sid Knight and is called the Black Bucktail.

Black Bucktail

Hooks	4 or 6 Kamasan B175
Silk	Black
Tail	Black bucktail hair
Body	Black floss
Rib	Oval silver
Hackle	(Body) Black cock hackle palmered over body
Hackle	(Head) Black cock hackle wound fully on behind the head and not at throat only
Wings	Black calf or bucktail tied sloping forward
Head	Black

Some dapping flies are bi-visible – the hackles used are a combination of dark ones and light ones. The advantage is that when the fly falls across a shaded part of the surface, under the shadow of a cloud for instance, or within the reflections from trees along the shore, the lighter hackles are more visible than the dark ones. When the fly falls across a bright surface the dark hackles are more visible. The fly is easily visible at all times, or at least that's the theory.

The Black Bucktail dapping fly.

Sid's Fore and Aft dapping fly.

Fore and Aft flies, that is flies with a hackle at each end, seem to carry better in a lighter wind. I have a particular liking for these, for no other reason than I caught the biggest sea trout I have ever caught while dapping on one – a fish of 6lb that I caught on Loch Hope. Again I am grateful to Sid Knight for the dressing.

Sid's Fore and Aft

Hook	Size 6 Kamasan B175
Silk	Brown
Tail	Natural brown bucktail hair
Body	Peacock herl wound thickly
Rib	Oval silver size 14
Hackle	(Rear) White cock hackle
Hackle	(Front) Natural red/brown cock hackle
Wing	White calf or bucktail tied sloping forward
Head	The brown silk varnished

Let me take you back to Loch Eck.

The day had gone quickly and it was about 5pm before I was back on the loch with the dapping rod set up. This time I fancied fishing along the west side of the loch under the shadow of Beinn Bheag. With a warm and steady breeze now blowing directly from the south I was sure to

get in a long drift without the need of too much boat handling. There was no longer any need for the drogue; the wind speed was just right to carry the boat on a more gentle drift. Although the waves were not quite so rough or as high as earlier, I still considered I had a chance of some good fishing.

I began to drift from a point by Bernice. With the rod held high, the wind picked up the blow-line perfectly. By lowering the rod, the Fore and Aft fly that I had on touched down and danced momentarily on the waves before it began to trip along the surface some fifteen feet ahead of the boat. No offer yet, but I felt sure that the action of the fly would soon attract a sea trout. The wind suddenly calmed for a while and the fly settled down on the surface. A sudden swirl, a rush of excitement, but no fish hooked. The secret of successful dapping is to keep the fly moving and not to let it settle too long on the water. The trick is to tempt fish by the action of the fly, which should appear as though it is about to fly away at any second. Let the fly settle on the water for too long and the fish will think it has all the time in the world. All too often I have watched sea trout come close or boil near a settled fly then turn away having examined it and decided that it wasn't quite the real thing. The fish must be tempted into thinking that it must take while the going is good or all will be lost.

As I raised the rod once more, another sudden gust of wind caught the line and held the fly suspended some eight inches or so over the surface. What happened next took me by surprise. A flash of silver shot straight out of the water and took the fly in mid air. It went straight to the bottom and then, the worst scenario afloat, it shot right under the boat. Playing a fish in these circumstances can be difficult. Apply too much pressure and the fish will be lost. Give it line and you still risk losing it.

The fish now rushed to the surface and leaped high in the air before crashing down with a mighty splash. I gave it line and prayed that the hook would hold. Fortunately it did, but I knew that it would only be a matter of time before I lost it if I didn't somehow manage to get the rod from under the boat. I scrambled to pass the rod around the bow and almost fell overboard when my foot caught in the strap of my fishing bag. By good fortune rather than skill the fish was still on and fighting with determination, but now I was in a better position to play it. At last I had it on a short line and was able to reach over the side with the waiting net. Eventually the fish turned on its side and I glided it in, but as it came over the net it found a new lease of life. It thrashed about and took off once again. But this time the fight was short lived and I soon had him in the net. It was one of the nicest sea trout I had ever seen, a specimen in every sense of the word, a beautifully proportioned bar of silver weighing just over 4lb with distinctive small blue crosses along its sides. This was a fish that I will always remember, as too was the day. Later, I caught five smaller sea trout on the dap before it was time to row the boat ashore, pack up my tackle and head for home.

Homeward bound.

Postscript

Now almost at the end of September, there was a distinctive nip in the fresh morning air; the sycamores and chestnuts were turning to red and gold and the sloe berries were blue and ripe. A thin veil of mist still clung to the river – autumn, it seemed, had arrived all too quickly. Just as it had in my life; so much I might have done, and didn't; so much I still need to do and so little time to do it in. Come spring and the trees would turn green and blossom once again, while I would only turn a little greyer. Another few days and the sea trout season would finally be over until next year. Perhaps I would have a cast or two for salmon in October or, then again, perhaps not. Along the edge of the wood I watched a squirrel busy burying hazel nuts, often a sign that we might be in for a severe winter. Perhaps this time there would be snow. We haven't had much of that in recent years, except on the peaks of the fells, and it would be nice to attend the Christmas carol service with snow on the ground and on the village church roof. I imagined the scene in the company of my family; excited grandchildren opening presents, mince pies and mulled wine, my wife's Christmas dinner – no one in the world can cook like Heather can. Perhaps winter would not be so bad after all. Starlings were gathering in large flocks and the sky was full of migrating geese. The river was fall of fish, both salmon and sea trout, most of which I presumed had come in on last week's ten-metre tides. I could make out the shadows of two large salmon lying against the wall of the pump house, per-

haps already preparing to spawn. I thought about calling on the keeper, who always makes a good cup of tea, and who I always enjoy having a chat with, but I changed my mind; I just had to get some work done.

Pausing by the weir, I thought about the pleasure I have had in writing this book and the new friends I have made in doing so. It never ceases to amaze me just how helpful people can be. The flies, the photographs, the wealth of information and time that I have been given has all served to make it worthwhile. I began to look back over the many years that I have spent in pursuit of sea trout. I had not always been successful. There were probably just as many times when I caught nothing at all, but it was all part of the journey and I have enjoyed many wonderful experiences and met some exceptional and interesting people along the way. This made me think of the time when I went to fish the River Towy and to take some photographs for this book. I fished all afternoon and all night until 6am in the company of that distinguished angler Gethyn Thomas, who is without doubt a great sewin fisherman. But on that occasion we failed to catch a single fish between the two of us. Gethyn is a man of great wit and generosity, and through the long night he told me about the time he had worked in the dank Welsh coal industry. We talked about our families, our children and grandchildren, our hopes and aspirations for them. I heard about his job as bailiff and the times when he had chased poachers. There was an amusing story about the seal that had swam up the river and how he and his helpers had tried to catch it. Under the canopy of stars, as two mere specks in the vast universe, we talked about the good times and the hard times in our lives, our sorrows and our joys. And as the night deepened, the conversation turned to politics and then to religion, philosophy and questions of belief. Somehow the catching of fish became of secondary importance as we shared our innermost thoughts in a way that people rarely do in this fast-track dog-eat-dog world. It seemed that in our own small way we had tried to make sense of all the problems in the world. The age we now live in, in which so much of that which is good and decent is ridiculed and scorned. The threat of global warming, which affects us all, and the particular impact this might have on the future, not just of fishing but of our fragile planet. The stupidity of mankind when we now have the wealth and technology to end so much suffering, famine and poverty. And yet the world is torn apart by greed and hatred, religious fanaticism, and the determination to get better and better at killing each other. What legacy do we leave to those who follow us?

Humanisation is a reciprocal thing. We cannot know ourselves or declare ourselves human unless we share in the humanity of another.

Brian Keenan
An Evil Cradling

Sadly, a good many of the pictures I took on the River Towy failed to come out. But as I continued along the river bank I began to think about what I had hoped to achieve by writing this book. Too many books which I have read on the subject of sea trout seem to me to be no more than rewrites of someone else's work or are frustratingly 'mechanical'. Some are so technical that the reader is blinded by science, which is something I have tried to avoid. I wanted to portray the subject through my own eyes and experiences – to take you fishing with me – perhaps in the hope that within these pages you might get to know me and share in my successes, as well as my failures. Had I missed out something important? Would some readers be writing to me to complain that I had not included this or that particular fly, or mentioned his or her own favourite fishing method? All these things went through my mind.

I thought about writing a chapter on the life cycle of the sea trout, then changed my mind. I'm not a scientist, I'm a fisherman. Others could write a study of the fish's natural history better than I and, besides, I didn't think that such a chapter would be read by many. As a writer, I know that most readers of fishing books simply want to get down to the brass tacks and the fishing, and that anyone wishing to delve deeper would get something more technical out of the library or look it up on the Internet. I reflected on the time when I worked on a painting of a Cornish fishing harbour. A point was finally reached when the composition looked very nice indeed and I was quietly satisfied with the way it had turned out. But then I started messing with it, adding a touch of colour here and another dab there and so on until I had completely spoilt the picture. How silly – I should have left well alone. I slowly began to feel as though a burden was beginning to lift from my shoulders. Yes, perhaps I had now written enough. The picture was painted. I could have gone on – I certainly have many more experiences and ideas that I would like to share with you, but in another book perhaps. This one ends here. I hope you enjoyed reading it.

The author (left) with Gethyn Thomas. We are discussing tactics on the bank of the River Towy. No fish were caught on this occasion, but the conversation more than made up for it.

Appendix I
Major UK Sea Trout Rivers

Listed below are the majority of noted sea trout rivers in the UK and Eire, and the best times when the presence of sea trout might be expected. It is, however, only an indication based on records over many years. Runs may vary from year to year depending on weather and river conditions. It is advisable to check the local starting and closing dates of the sea trout season.

ENGLAND

River	Lower reaches	Upper reaches
Avon (Devon)	June to Aug	June to Aug
Avon (Hampshire)	June and July	—
Calder (Cumbria)	June to Sept	July to Sept
Camel	July and Aug	July and Aug
Coquet	Sept and Oct	Sept and Oct
Dart	July to Sept	July to Sept
Derwent (Cumbria)	June to Sept	June to Sept
Duddon	July and Aug	July and Aug
Eden	May to Sept	May to Sept
Esk (Border)	May to Sept	May to Sept
Esk (Cumbria)	July to Sept	July to Sept
Fowey	July and Aug	July and Aug
Frome (Dorset)	July and Aug	July and Aug
Hodder	July to Sept	July to Sept
Irt	July to Sept	July to Sept
Itchen	June and July	—
Kent	July and Aug	July and Aug
Leven	July and Aug	July to Sept
Looe	July and Aug	July and Aug

Lune	June to Sept	June to Sept
Piddle	June and July	June and July
Plym	July and Aug	July and Aug
Ribble	June to Sept	July to Sept
Stour	June and July	—
Tamar	July and Aug	July and Aug
Tavy	July and Aug	July and Aug
Taw	June to Sept	June to Sept
Tees	June to Aug	Aug to Sept
Teign	June to Sept	June to Sept
Test	June and July	—
Torridge	June to Sept	June to Sept
Tyne	June to Aug	Aug and Sept
Wear	June to Aug	Aug and Sept
Yealm	July and Aug	July and Aug

SCOTLAND

River	Lower reaches	Upper reaches
Annan	April to July	April to July
Awe	May to Aug	May to Aug
Beauly	April, May, July	July to Oct
Brora	May, June and Sept	June and July
Dee	June and July	—
Deveron	June and July	June and July
Doon	Sept and Oct	Sept and Oct
Esk (South)	June onwards	June onwards
Ewe	July to Oct	July to Oct
Findhorn	—	April and May
Forth	—	May and June
Nith	April to July	April to July
Oykel	July onwards	July onwards
Spey	April to May	April to June
Stinchar	July to Sept	July to Sept
Tay	Aug to Oct	Aug to Oct

River	Lower reaches	Upper reaches
Tweed	Mid July to late Aug	Mid July to late Aug
Ugie	June to Oct	June to Oct
Ythan	June to Oct	June to Oct

WALES

River	Lower reaches	Upper reaches
Conwy	June onwards	June onwards
Clwyd	May to Oct	Sept to Oct
Dovey	June onwards	Aug onwards
Glaslyn	Late July and Aug	Late July and Aug
Lledr	June onwards	June onwards
Mawddach	June to Sept	June to Sept
Teifi	July onwards	—
Towy	June onwards	July onwards
Usk	Aug and Sept	Aug and Sept

NORTHERN IRELAND

River	Lower reaches	Upper reaches
Bann	Aug and Sept	—
Finn	June onwards	June onwards
Foyle and tributaries (excluding Finn)	June onwards	June onwards
Faughan	June onwards	June onwards
Roe	June onwards	June onwards

EIRE

River	Lower reaches	Upper reaches
Ballynahinch	July to Oct	—
Bandon	Feb to April	April to June
Blackwater	June onwards	June onwards
Boyne	June onwards	—
Bundrowes	July and Aug	July and Aug
Burrieshoole	July to Sept	July to Sept
Caragh	July onwards	July onwards

Cashla	June to Oct	June to Oct
Clare-Galway	June onwards	June onwards
Comb	June onwards	June onwards
Clady	Aug and Sept	Aug and Sept
Erne	July and Aug	—
Erriff	July to Oct	July to Oct
Feale	June onwards	June onwards
Gweebarra	Late June to Sept	Late June to Sept
Laune	April to Sept	April to Sept
Lee	Feb and March	April and May
Leannan	June onwards	June onwards
Maine	Aug and Sept	Aug and Sept
Moy	June onwards	June onwards
Newport	July to Sept	July to Sept
Owenduff	Late June onwards	Late June onwards
Owenea	July to Sept	July to Sept
Owengarve	July to Sept	July to Sept
Owengowla	June to Oct	June to Oct
Owenmore	Mid June to Sept	Mid June to Sept
Slaney	June to Aug	June to Aug
Waterville	July to Oct	July to Oct

The Snake Fly is gaining a reputation as a taker of salmon in the night. These two fresh 14lb salmon were taken by the author on the River Esk (Border) while fishing for sea trout in low summer conditions. Both fish were taken between 2 and 3am on a $2^1/_2$in Blue and Silver Snake dressed with a phosphorescent Mylar tube body.

Appendix II
Recommended Partridge Hooks

The hooks listed below are those recommended by the author in the dressing of sea trout flies, and are reproduced by kind permission of Partridge of Redditch.

01. Single Wilson Hooks

N. Single Low-Water Hooks

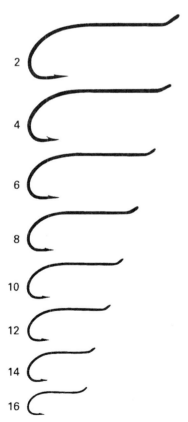

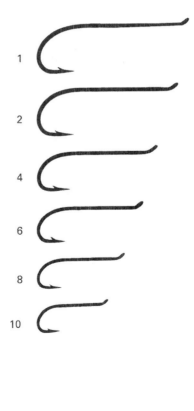

RECOMMENDED PARTRIDGE HOOKS

CS14/1 B, S, G. Salar

CS10/1. Bartleet Single Hooks

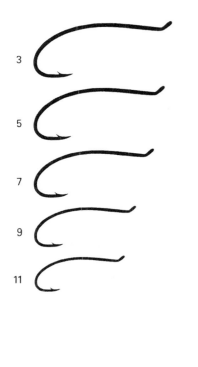

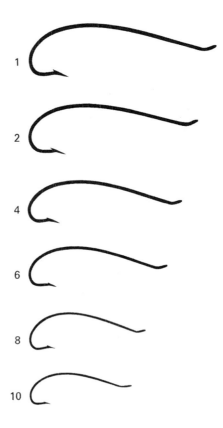

CS10/2. Bartleet Supreme Fly Hooks   02. Double Wilson Hooks

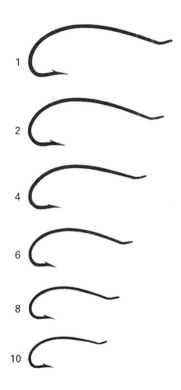

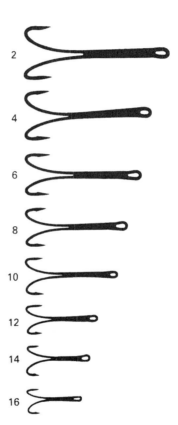

Q. Double Low-Water Hooks

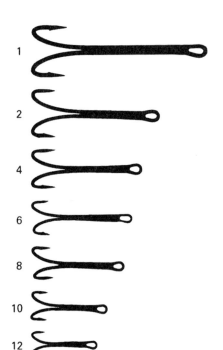

CS10/4. Bartleet Double Hooks

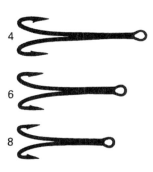

CS14/2 B, S, G. Salar Double Salmon

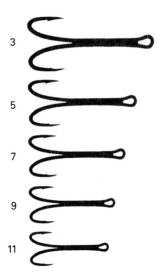

CS14T/2. B, S, G. Salar. Tube Doubles

RIA. Double Limerick Hooks

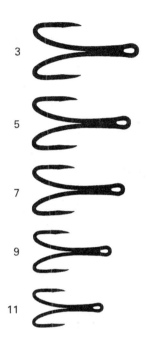

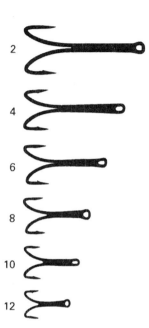

R2A. Outpoint Double Hooks

XIBR/X1BL/GRSXI. Standard Treble Hooks

X2B. Long Shank Treble Hooks

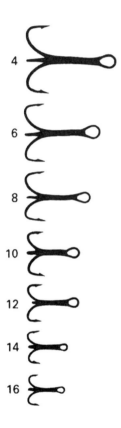

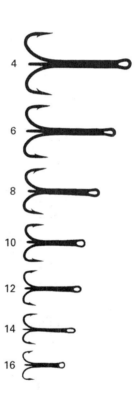

CS12. 6X Long Shank Treble Hooks

X3BL. Needle Eye Tube Fly Treble Hooks

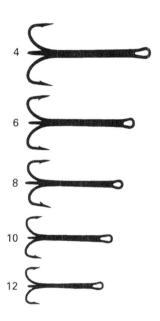

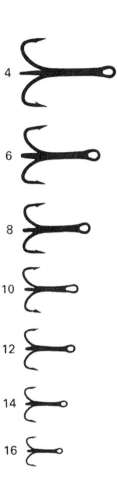

RECOMMENDED PARTRIDGE HOOKS

V1B. Double Waddington Shanks   15BN. Klinkhamer

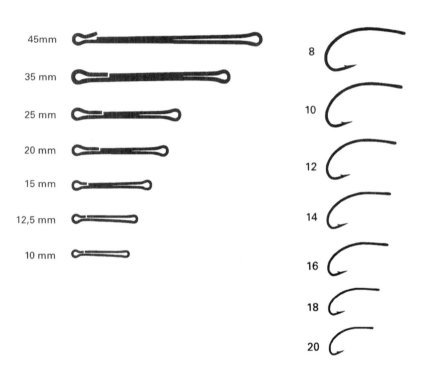

R2A. Outpoint Double Hooks

D4AF. Bucktail/Streamer Hooks

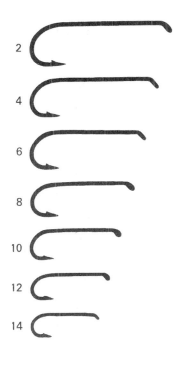

CS52. Sea Prince Saltwater Fly Hook

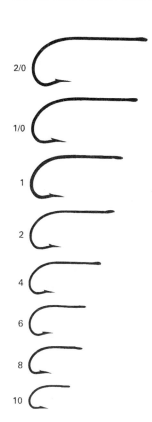

YL2A. Captain Hamilton Wet Fly Hooks

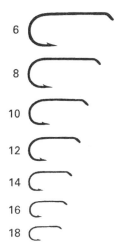

The author fishing on the Cumbrian Esk, the home of the 'Medicine'.

Appendix III
Flies and Fly Dressings

Fishing for sea trout on the lower Ribble.

INDEX